The Armed Self-Defense Handbook

American Concealed

Jon Archer
Jason Alva

Copyright © 2017 by American Concealed, Inc.

All rights reserved. This book or any portion thereof may not be reproduced or used in any manner whatsoever without the express written permission of the publisher except for the use of brief quotations in a book review.

Created in the United States of America

First Edition, 2017

For permission and ordering information, contact American Concealed, Inc. with the information listed below. Special discounts are available on quantity purchases.

American Concealed, Inc.
207 East 5th Avenue, Suite 224
Eugene, OR 97401
www.americanconcealed.com

Contents

INTRODUCTION

Part One: What Everyone Should Know About Carrying Concealed...1
3 Questions You Must Ask Yourself Before Carrying Concealed...4
The Truth Behind Popular Concealed Carry Myths...9
Building a Foundation of Handgun Safety...12

Part Two: How to Carry Concealed...17
Holster Basics...19
Methods of Concealed Carry...23
The Location of Your Concealed Carry Handgun...24
Carrying a Backup CCW...30
Tactical Gear for Concealed Carry...32
Using Hollow Point Ammunition for Self-Defense...40
How to Choose a Caliber for Concealed Carry...42
Carrying Concealed in Warm Weather...43
Carrying Concealed in Cold Weather...45
Carrying Concealed in the Workplace...47
Carrying Concealed in the Classroom...48
Carrying Concealed on Campus...50

Part Three: The Fundamentals of Defensive Shooting...55
Defensive Body Positions...57
Gun Grip in Defensive Firing...58
Trigger Squeeze...60
Sight Alignment...62
What is Knockdown Power?...64

Part Four: Preventing and Surviving Self-Defense Scenarios...67
Turn the Tables with Situational Awareness...68
How to Stay Calm in Combat...71
What Happens Inside Your Body During a Violent Attack?...74

Contents

Consider the Many Options for Personal Protection.........................75
Preventing a Home Invasion..79
What Intruders Look For When Choosing a Home to Invade................81
What to Do When There's an Intruder in Your Home............................83
What to Do in an Armed Robbery..85
How to Survive an Active Shooter...86
What to Do if You're Attacked In or Near Your Car...............................88
How to Carry Concealed in Bars and Restaurants..............................90

Part Five: The Legal Aspects of Self-Defense.........................93
What to Do After an Armed Self-Defense Incident..............................94
The Judicious Use of Deadly Force..97
The Castle Doctrine, Duty to Retreat, and Stand Your Ground............99

Part Six: Skill Building and Practice.......................................104
Build Muscle Memory for Increased Accuracy and Effectiveness..........105
Make the Most of Your Practice at the Firing Range..........................106
Preparing for Firing Range Practice..109
Analyzing Your Draw Sequence..111
Cartridge Malfunctions and How to Handle Them Safely..................113

Conclusion...115

Additional Resources..117

Acknowledgements

To Those Who Made This Book Possible,

Our world today demands that its citizens be informed, alert, and armed. That makes writing a book like this one easy. American citizens are eager to learn, train, and take their rights very seriously.

The rest of this project wouldn't have gotten off the ground without dedication and effort from a very supportive team.

A special thanks goes to Shaylor Murray, Roger Leach, and Jefferson Leach for their talent and dedication to providing people with high-quality training materials. To Michael, Vaughn, Vanessa, and Steve for their crucial information and suggestions on overall design and graphic elements.

And a special thanks to all of the loyal readers of American Concealed for exchanging your hard-earned money in order to learn how to protect the people of this great country.

Introduction

The decision to carry concealed is one of the most important choices you'll make in your life. A concealed handgun enables you to protect yourself and others from the most deadly harm imaginable, but it carries with it immense responsibility.

Despite their glorified role in television, movies, and music, handguns are weapons that should be respected and treated with tremendous caution. It is your responsibility to care for and use a concealed handgun in a way that is responsible and dignified.

If you've decided to carry concealed, congratulations. You've stepped forward to become a responsible citizen armed for protection. If you've been carrying for many years, you may assume that you aren't in need of practice or don't need to refresh yourself on the current laws for your state. This is a mistake.

Everyone should take the time to inform themselves of current concealed carry legislation, strategies for care and handling of firearms, and proper self-defense techniques. This information applies to those who have been carrying concealed for years, just a few days, and even individuals who have never handled a firearm.

We've filled this guidebook with the essential information regarding carrying a concealed handgun. There's no fluff or unnecessary stories to fill up the pages or entertain you. This guidebook is not a substitute for regular practice or legal advice. What we present here are actions you must take on your own in order to become a more responsible and judicious gun owner.

Read this guidebook and use it as a companion to your firearms training. Use this book to instruct your family or friends in how to carry concealed or to answer their questions about why you made the decision to arm yourself. New gun owners and seasoned shooters alike should keep this guidebook as a reference and refresher.

At American Concealed, we take gun ownership and the responsibility of carrying concealed very seriously. We dedicate our work and our efforts to teaching individuals the proper methods of concealed carry. We understand that we have been granted a right to defend ourselves with a firearm, and we encourage others to take full advantage of this right.

We also know that anyone who misuses a firearm or takes their right for granted may be a danger to themselves or others. It is the individual responsibility of every gun owner to practice proper technique, understand the moral and legal elements of concealed carry, and possess a detailed knowledge of the parts and function of various firearms and accessories.

We hope you enjoy reading this concealed carry guidebook and find the information helpful. We hope to inspire you to practice more frequently and to be a model for responsible gun ownership.

Part One

What Everyone Should Know Before Carrying Concealed

American Concealed

Self-defense is a basic human right. Over the course of history, humans have proven to be a tough bunch, ready and able to defend themselves should danger arise. While the tools we've used to do so have certainly changed over the years, the point has always stayed the same. When another person is acting in a way that threatens our life, us humans have shown a tremendous capacity for courage.

Citizens of the United States are fortunate to live with a government built from a Constitution and Bill of Rights created with the best interest of the people in mind. The Second Amendment to the United States Constitution was adopted in 1791, and protects the right of the people to keep and bear arms.

In 2008, the Supreme Court of the United States considered the landmark case District of Columbia v. Heller, 554 U.S. 570. In a 5-4 decision, they held that the Second Amendment applied to individuals and protects their right to possess a firearm, outside of a militia, for lawful purposes. Self-defense is considered to be one of those lawful purposes. The Second Amendment has endured this and numerous other intense examinations and criticisms from all angles, and will continue to be challenged and discussed for many years to come.

It certainly didn't happen overnight, but now all 50 states consider the lawful concealed carry of a firearm to be an accepted method of self-defense as it was represented in the Bill of Rights and in more recent Supreme Court decisions. Debate still continues as to the finer points of concealed carry; regulations concerning gun-free zones, interstate reciprocity, and required permits vary from state to state. These issues aside, the responsible and lawful carry of a concealed handgun is, and will be for the foreseeable future, an accepted practice.

One of the main reasons that the practice has received such wide acceptance is that the basic principles are simple. Carrying a firearm for self-defense doesn't need to be a complicated issue. If you learn and master the foundation of responsible and judicious carry the act will become second nature.

There are, however, some very real threats to this attitude of acceptance. These may not be easy to see outright, but evidence of their existence can be seen in countless online videos, blog posts, photos, and online forums. Buying and using firearms is definitely a fun and engaging hobby, but when image becomes more important than safety the odds that guns are abused increase.

For starters, the best way to increase and strengthen the acceptance of concealed carry is to encourage and promote training, regular education, and lawful practices. Knowing the applicable laws, learning and practicing correct handling, and carrying with a serious, positive attitude all go a long way to promote armed self-defense. In the following chapters, we'll outline what equipment, strategies, and techniques are required to carry concealed for armed self-defense.

You might think that purchasing a firearm is the first step in concealed carry. In fact, a few things should happen well before you buy your first gun. Asking yourself some serious questions about the moral, social, and legal responsibilities of concealed carry should be the very first step. Have this conversation with yourself and with your family and close friends. In many cases, they will be nearby when you need to use your concealed firearm for protection. Their thoughts on the issues are important to consider.

After you're aware of these issues and you've made a firm decision to take on the increased responsibility, start reviewing your options in order to purchase the best gun, holster, and tactical gear for you. There are many factors to consider depending on your lifestyle, body type, and specific needs. A firearm is a serious and expensive purchase, so choose wisely.

The act of self-defense, armed or not, is brutal and traumatizing. If a life-threatening event happens to you, odds are good that the attacker will be someone you know, in a place where you frequent. If not, the attack will likely take place quickly and without warning. There are many ways to prevent these violent situations and keep yourself safe, so there's no need to walk around in fear of what may be hiding around every corner.

It's also worth learning about what happens to your brain and your body when these attacks take place. Knowing what to expect and how to handle your body's natural reactions to fear and pain can help you to defend yourself quickly and effectively. The biggest mistake you can make in self-defense is thinking that it could never happen to you.

Finally, you'll need to learn and regularly practice the safe handling of a firearm. This isn't something that only new gun owners do, it's a necessary action for all gun owners no matter how experienced. It's the responsibility of every gun owner to learn and practice safe and responsible firearm use.

3 Questions You Must Ask Yourself Before Carrying Concealed

These questions are listed at the beginning of this book for a reason. They're here to make sure that each and every person who reads this understands that carrying concealed is a serious responsibility. Everyone, from experienced security professionals to first-time gun owners, should be totally clear on the implications of armed self-defense.

That's right. Everyone who carries responsibly considers the impact of their actions each and every time they holster a weapon. It's not just about causing serious injury or death either. It's a consideration of the higher standard of responsibility to which people who carry firearms are held. Medical professionals, law enforcement officers, and teachers are just a few examples of people who are held to a high standard of excellence at work, and those jobs are definitely not for everyone. You should take the time to consider if you can handle the responsibility that comes with carrying concealed.

Armed self-defense may be one of our constitutional rights as Americans, but that doesn't mean that everyone should do it.

Anyone unable to confidently answer these questions should think twice before stepping out the door with a concealed firearm. The consequences of poor use are simply too serious. Concealed carry is not about popularity or toughness. If you're carrying, it is no time for fun or for trying to imitate your favorite action hero.

If you're carrying concealed, you should be prepared for anything. You have decided to protect yourself and others with your handgun should the need arise, so it pays to be sure you know what it takes. It's never as simple as just drawing your gun and pulling the trigger to kill the bad guy. The situation will always be much more complicated. Every violent situation brings with it complicated legal and personal issues. The responsibility to understand these rules and actions lies with the gun owner, not with any other person or entity. Every gun owner should be able to answer these questions without hesitation.

In what locations do I carry concealed?

The more often you carry concealed, the more comfortable you'll be. But you can never just grab your gun and go. Depending on where you live, there are a variety of places where guns are forbidden. Review your state and local laws about schools, college campuses, and government offices. Know the locations of "Gun Free Zones" in your community. The Gun Free School Zones Act became an official federal United States law back in 1990. It prohibits unauthorized people from carrying a firearm on any property that is defined as a school zone.

Generally, this refers to any public, private, or parochial school and can extend up to 1,000 feet off the property. Some states allow carry on these properties with an official license or permit, while others allow the local municipalities to decide the rules. There are always exceptions to the law, however, so research the exact guidelines for your particular state of residence.

The effectiveness and constitutionality of gun free zones has been debated fiercely over recent years, and many states continue to review these laws in consideration of the safety of the citizens. Community colleges and universities, for instance, have different ideas about just where concealed carry is permitted. Some campuses may permit students to carry concealed while others require that firearms be locked in cars in the parking lot.

Gun free zones do not only apply to schools. Locations that hold any state or local government offices, post offices, libraries, civic centers, sports arenas, and parks are sometimes considered gun free zones. It's best to take it upon yourself to be informed about where concealed carry is permitted, and not rely on posted signs or security to inform you of the regulations.

Absent-mindedness and concealed carry do not mix, and carrying in unauthorized areas can lead to substantial fines and criminal charges. This only reinforces the fact that responsible concealed carry requires a dedication to understanding the laws of your local community.

Aside from the physical locations you may encounter while carrying concealed, it is also important that you consider the people and situations that you'll encounter during the day. Sadly, our dedication to safe and responsible concealed carry is not enough to sway the opinions of some of our fellow citizens.

Gun ownership is a divisive issue in our society, and people are entitled to hold their own opinions, no matter how much we might disagree with them. On the other hand, you may also encounter individuals who would like nothing better than to separate you from your firearm for their own financial gain. When you're considering concealed carry, remember that those people will be nearby anywhere you are likely to find yourself. This is why we must put considerable emphasis on the word "concealed" in this case.

The situations you may encounter while carrying concealed can vary greatly. Carrying to the office on a quiet workday holds different potential circumstances than carrying at an outdoor market.

It's your responsibility to conceal your firearm appropriately and to also know how to handle it if you need to defend yourself. In these cases it isn't the legality of carry that is necessarily the issue, but the responsible use of a firearm should the need arise. Before carrying in situations like this, you must be informed of proper target identification, the use of deadly force, and firing stances.

The main issue is this: You never know just what situations you might encounter during the day. All you can do is prepare as best you can. Think about what types of people you might encounter or the stores you'll be shopping in during the day. Be aware of your surroundings and situations that might require you to protect yourself.

Am I familiar with federal, state, and local laws concerning transporting and carrying a concealed weapon?

There's a lot more to carrying concealed than a handgun and holster. You must have a good understanding of the laws and regulations for the transportation of firearms. Air travel, car travel, and carrying across state lines are all issues that gun owners should be aware of.

It takes some research to learn how each state handles the issue, but obeying these laws can save you money and legal problems down the road.

Transporting your firearm on an airline can be a very easy process. Do it incorrectly and you're in for a very long day. Review the guidelines and do your research so that air travel with a firearm is easy and smooth.

Find out how to transport your gun in your car when you're going to and from the range. Regulations vary from state to state as to where it can be kept and how the gun should be secured.

We're all taught that members of law enforcement are in place to protect and serve, but carrying concealed can add a different element to the conversation. If it's just a routine traffic stop or if it's after you've used your firearm for protection, you must know just how to act and what phrases to use when you come into contact with law enforcement.

Become familiar with your legal rights and just what you can say and do with law enforcement present. It could end up saving you frustration and legal fees.

When was the last time I practiced shooting, loading, and cleaning my handgun?

Throughout this book, we'll touch on these three fundamentals of concealed carry, and gun ownership in general. The fact of the matter is, concealed carry is pointless if the carrier and firearm are not in good working order. In order to be most effective, the person carrying the handgun should be informed, confident, and emotionally prepared for armed self-defense.

Like a hand in a glove, carrier and handgun should go perfectly together. The handgun must be clean and in good working order. If one is not functioning correctly, the whole system is ineffective.

Keeping up with regular cleaning and maintenance of your guns has benefits. Regular cleanings obviously keep your handgun in peak performance by eliminating any dirt or particles that may result from frequent carry. When you purchase your firearm, read the directions for proper care and maintenance.

This purchase isn't like anything else you've ever owned. The way that it functions and the way you take care of it has a direct impact on your safety. Regular cleaning and proper handling should become a bit of an obsession, and the importance cannot be overstated.

Just as the state of your home shows a lot about the type of person you are, the cleanliness of your firearm shows just how dedicated you are to safe and responsible gun ownership.

It also helps you to become more familiar with the mechanics of your gun so that you're better able to fix minor problems yourself and teach others the same skills. Regular practice is one of the essential elements of gun ownership.

Practice keeps your confidence high and your physical skills sharp. When the situation calls for armed self-defense, your handgun should be an extension of yourself. Regular trips to the range alone or with friends are the only way to keep improving your aim, draw, and technical skill.

If you had any trouble answering any of these questions, take some time and get familiar with the facts. A responsible and trained citizen armed for self-defense goes a long way to keeping our country a safe place to live.

Concealed carry requires more than just knowledge and skill. It takes a person who is aware of the responsibility that comes with gun ownership. A responsible gun owner has thought for a long time and considered the many costs and benefits to concealed carry. They've asked themselves and their family some tough questions, and they're prepared for any situation.

The Truth Behind Popular Concealed Carry Myths

There are many misconceptions out there about carrying concealed handguns for protection. When this false information spreads, people start to form negative opinions based on it. This misinformation can lead to problems in the form of arguments, increased regulations from political groups, and feelings of resentment within the gun community.

When you choose to carry concealed, you've taken on the responsibility of spreading positive truth about yourself as a gun owner. When people act irresponsibly and in ways that aren't respectful of those who disagree, myths and negative opinions spread.

When a gun owner acts foolishly and hurts themselves or another innocent person, they only keep the myths alive. You can help to fight these by carrying a firearm responsibly and by keeping safety and training a top priority.

Myth #1: The only people who carry concealed are old guys who live out in the sticks.

There is a stereotype that Americans who carry guns for protection are just old conservative white guys in rural areas. The media is pretty effective at portraying gun owners as thoughtless conservatives who love nothing more than firing at anything that moves. The truth is much different.

Recent surveys have shown increasing numbers of women that own guns. The number of women who go hunting has increased 85% since 2001 and the number of female target shooters increased 60%. Not only are there increasing numbers of women gun owners, but they're safe and certified as well. According to the National Shooting Sports Foundation, 73% of female gun owners have taken at least one firearms training class and 43% of them go target shooting at least once a month.

Certified firearms instructors have been reporting over the past few years that they're witnessing big increases in the number of women and minorities who are attending their classes. Urban areas such as Detroit are experiencing an uptick in registered gun ownership. This increase in law-abiding citizens owning firearms has resulted in a decrease in violent incidents like robbery, carjacking, and break-ins.

Myth #2: Concealed carry will turn America into the Wild West.

There is this idea out there that more citizens armed for self-defense will result in shootouts in the street, road rage killings, and more violent crime in general. It's important to remember that there's a difference between lawfun gun owners that carry concealed for self-defense and criminals that knowlingly use a firearm to commit violent crimes.

According to FBI crime statistics over the past few years, violent crimes like murder and non-negligent manslaughter, rape, robbery, and aggravated assualt all rise and fall regularly. Regardless of the year, violent criminal activity is now a fact of life for people all over the country. Research shows that the perpetrators of these violent crimes are not the same people that are carrying concealed.

Last year the Crime Prevention Research Center reported that there are over 14.5 million concealed handgun permits, a 215% increase since 2007. This research suggests that concealed carry permit holders are often law abiding citizens and commit less crimes compared to the general population and even compared to police officers.

The truth is that more and more people in America are choosing to arm themselves with a concealed handgun for self-defense. People of many different geographic origins, social backgrounds, races, and ages are deciding to take personal safety into their own hands. This doesn't mean that they are using the guns for nefarious purposes.

Largely, they obey the laws of the state and country in which they live. They attend certification classes and hold legal permits to own and carry firearms.

The best way to continue to prove these myths incorrect is to continue to be (and influence younger generations to be) responsible, safe, and practiced gun owners. Practice regularly, obtain proper certification, and demonstrate all of the safety precautions necessary to keep yourself and your loved ones secure.

American Concealed

Building a Foundation of Handgun Safety

There is much more to concealed carry than a holster, a handgun, and ammo. Just as you should be able to handle the responsibility and tough choices that come with armed self-defense, you should also know the safety rules that bind it all together. Handgun safety is just like every other skill a person learns. It starts with a solid foundation and stays sharp through regular practice.

First and foremost, safe handling of a firearm requires your undivided attention. When a gun is in your hands, you stop the other things you're doing and concentrate on handling it properly. The goal should always be to keep yourself and everyone around you safe and secure. Target shooting, hunting, and tactical practice is a great way to socialize with friends, but one second of thoughtless action and the fun is over.

Why is safety the foundation of armed self-defense? Shouldn't your aim, trigger squeeze, or your ammunition be the central part in using a gun for protection? The reason that safety is the foundation is because it is the base from which all other skills grow. Just like the trunk of a tree supports all of the branches and leaves that extend outward, safe firearm practices are the backbone of every tactical maneuver in armed self-defense.

Some who are very experienced with concealed carry might find the endless safety measures to be tedious. They may think that their experiences with firearms give them a higher level of safety than the novice. These false ideas can be destroyed in the blink of an eye. Don't let these people fool you into thinking that firearm professionals, security experts, and long-time gun hobbyists don't need to practice protective safety measures.

If you have built and maintained a solid foundation of safety, you are better able to build a very large array of different shooting and self-defense skills. Complicated maneuvers, shooting stances, and more sophisticated firearms all require that the shooter master some basic safety skills.

Don't be fooled though, this doesn't mean that once you've learned them you can abandon the practices. First they become a habit, then a lifestyle.

Have a positive attitude.

If you asked a thousand handgun owners about the essential elements of handgun safety, odds are good that only a few of them would ever mention a positive attitude. Think about what controls the actions of your hands, fingers, and even your toes. It's your brain.

What about the things you do without thinking, like breathing or digesting those pancakes you had for breakfast? Your brain controls those too. The power of a positive attitude (and the consequences of a negative attitude) are frequently overlooked, and for that reason we've made it our first rule of handgun safety.

Negative emotions like anger and depression can lead to misuse of handguns. Don't underestimate the power of your thoughts and how they can influence your actions. You're more likely to be impulsive, act out physically, and show less care for others when you feel down.

When you're armed for self-defense, take stock of what's going through your mind. Are you angry at someone, or even yourself? Has it been a long day at work or a frustrating night at home? These situations will pass and anger won't last. You have the chance to make things right. If things are not going well for you, and it happens to everyone from time to time, don't handle or carry a firearm.

When you do, the chances of an accident or making a very poor choice increase tremendously. Take some time to collect yourself and get a good hold on how you're feeling. A concealed handgun is for protection against a threat that might end your life, not for solving problems that make you angry. A calm and collected mental state will result in better decision making.

Sadly, drugs and alcohol often go hand in hand with negative emotions. Even when things start out as a happy celebration, these substances have the ability to alter your thoughts and reactions, making it much more likely that you'll make bad choices.

There is simply no place for alcohol or other drugs when firearms are in the picture. If the warning about potentially destroying yourself or others accidentally isn't enough to convince you, consider what the courts will say. If you use your concealed handgun for self-defense but law enforcement officers report that you were under the influence of a substance, you may end up losing a costly legal battle.

Drugs and bad attitudes from negative circumstances often come up in the courtroom as evidence. If an attorney can demonstrate that your actions were influenced by these things you could be headed for a world of legal trouble.

Be a student of the gun.

If you were raised in a household that encouraged hunting and recreational shooting, you've probably already gotten a great start at practicing handgun safety. If someone taught you how to respect and use all types of firearms, you're fortunate to have had such a good role model. But don't let this fool you into thinking that you've learned all there is to learn about guns and how to use them.

We might think that many years of carrying concealed, target practice, and hunting have taught us all we need to know. Some might think that reading and learning about handgun laws, gun technology, and current issues is only for new gun owners.

The truth is, we all must become students of the gun. Carrying concealed means that you're taking your life and the lives of others into your hands. There is great power and responsibility in this.

Keep up with handgun blogs and publications. Participate in discussions about gun issues respectfully and consider the viewpoints of others. Your ability to talk about carrying concealed in an intelligent way will do a lot for promoting a positive image of concealed carry. Building your knowledge will also result in better respect for guns and therefore better safety.

Develop a specific set of skills.

Before we start discussing the skills you need for armed self-defense, let's first remember that knowledge and skills are two very different things. Someone can talk for hours about the history of baseball and current statistics but not be able to hit a baseball with a bat to save his life. Knowing the names and calibers of all the most famous handguns doesn't mean that you'll know how to operate one effectively.

As handgun owners, it's up to us to demonstrate safe and practiced firearm use. The best way to build those skills is through constant practice. This fact can't be repeated enough.

Our muscles and brains learn to move quickly and efficiently only through building muscle memory. The way to do this is practice movements over and over again.

Everyone who is armed with a handgun for self-defense must start off every practice session, and each day they carry concealed, with a safety routine. It doesn't matter if you're alone or with others, at home or at work, the routine of safety never changes. As you determine that your weapon is safe to handle, talk to yourself to enforce the fact that you are doing what needs to be done to ensure the safety of yourself and everyone around you.

Time spent practicing at the range is vital to being prepared when the time comes to use your concealed weapon. There are plenty of options and ways to practice even while you're at home. Involving your family is another way to not only practice, but also be a positive role model to young people.

In future chapters we'll discuss ways to make your time at the range really pay off, but for now let's reinforce the fact that practice is a central element of armed self-defense. Most importantly, your range training must focus on skills that apply to real-life self-defense situations. A violent attacker will not give you time to adjust your firing stance or give you a minute while you struggle with your pocket holster. Some relaxed firing for fun is certainly fine, but practicing for specific scenarios is an absolute must.

Gun owners must realize and respect that they are ambassadors for armed self-defense in America. Demonstrating proper technique and safety precautions shows children how to respect firearms. It also shows our friends, family, and other citizens that when it comes to guns, there really isn't anything to fear. It's the person behind the gun that we should be aware of.

When they're used without respect and training, guns can cause serious destruction. If the person using doesn't have a positive attitude or adequate safety training, get out of there as quickly as you can.

A foundation of safety starts small. From the time we pick up and handle our first firearm to the time we buy and carry our own, we must have respect for its potential for protection. If we want other people and our government representatives to share our passion and respect for armed self-defense, it starts with our personal practices. We do have the constitutional right to own firearms, but doing so safely and responsibly is what really gives us power.

Part Two

How to Carry Concealed

American Concealed

There's more to concealed carry than simply owning a firearm for self-defense. Armed self-defense is most effective after training and research into just what a firearm is capable of. The process of obtaining your permit and handgun is relatively easy and fast, but actually learning the correct strategies for carrying concealed takes much more time and effort.

There are three distinct areas of concealed carry tactics, and it's crucial that everyone that's armed for self-defense understand each one. They all work together to make concealed carry a safe practice for everyone.

First, choose the correct gear and equipment. There's plenty to choose from out there, and it's up to you to try everything before making the commitment to what you'll use each and every day when you carry concealed.

Second, understand the legal aspects of concealed carry and firearm ownership where you live and travel. Every state treats the permit process differently, and it's your responsibility to understand and be informed about where and when carrying a firearm is permitted.

Lastly, train and learn more about armed self-defense every chance you get. Even the most experienced gun owners must review every step of the process regularly to ensure that they're on top of their game. You can always learn more, and never think that you're above regular training and practice.

Holster Basics

Armed self-defense simply doesn't happen without a proper holster. There are as many choices for a holster as there are handguns, so the decision-making process is one that should take time and research. Just as each person should select a defensive handgun based on their lifestyle and personal needs, a concealed carry holster is a very personalized purchase.

Carrying the incorrect holster can have some unexpected negative results. Poorly fitting holsters are downright dangerous in fact. You wouldn't make a significant and expensive purchase of clothes without first trying the item on and considering how you'd wear it, but holster purchases are often quick affairs based on little research. This can usually be chalked up to a new gun owner's desire to impress friends or store owners by not asking many questions or testing the gear.

For this reason, many handgun owners are not using the correct concealed carry holster. When some clothing item doesn't fit comfortably, it's easy to return and doesn't cause much concern or pain. Not so with a concealed carry holster.

If you continue to carry after you feel the holster doesn't fit correctly, the mistake could have fatal consequences. Let's take a look at some guidelines to be sure that you're using the correct holster for concealed carry.

Only use handgun holsters with trigger protection.

Trigger protection is one of the top safety considerations when choosing a holster. Engaging the trigger accidentally is without question a serious mistake that can have deadly and seriously embarrassing consequences. Even with all legal bases covered and plenty of regular training, accidental discharge resulting from an incorrect holster means damage beyond repair.

No matter how perfectly it feels or how highly another gun owner recommends it, do not use a holster that doesn't provide adequate trigger coverage.

If you're using the correct concealed carry holster, you'll see that it protects the trigger from getting caught on clothing. If the gun needs to be drawn quickly the trigger should not be in danger of snags in a pocket, belt, or purse. Before you purchase a holster, think very seriously about your lifestyle and what clothing or accessories you'll be wearing while you're carrying concealed. A holster should meet the demands of everything, everyone, and every place you'll encounter throughout the day. No matter the movement or the clothes, your holster should keep the gun from ever being caught on a jacket, purse strap, or items in your pockets.

This is why you should weigh the reviews of others very lightly when choosing a holster. Odds are good that they don't go to the same places, wear the same clothing styles, or have the same performance requirements as you.

One other item to consider in a holster's trigger protection is finger access. One of the main rules of gun ownership is that your finger should never be on the trigger unless there is intent to destroy. Your trigger finger is always on the frame of the handgun until you feel that you have no other choice but to fire. That being said, any holster that allows your trigger finger to get near the trigger while drawing should be avoided.

A quality concealed carry holster helps keep your fingers in the correct place while drawing while also keeping the gun secure. Special consideration should be given for pocket holsters and hip holsters featuring any slide or press feature that is meant to increase security.

Only choose safe and secure concealed carry holsters.

The ability to access a defensive firearm in a secure holster quickly and safely is a top priority. The holster you choose for armed self-defense should not be a discount brand or one that was previously worn by someone else. It shouldn't be one that you buy for looks or because a friend uses it. Your hands, body, and clothes are different from everyone else, so choose a holster that stays secure for you.

Concealed carry holsters should be accessible in a variety of circumstances. Armed self-defense is very different from target practice at the firing range. At the range, everything is very safe and regulated. You have plenty of time to reload, breathe, and aim as precisely as possible. An attack that threatens your life will be fast and painful, with very little time to think over your options and aim.

The speed and the effectiveness that's required in a deadly encounter makes the fit and security of your armed self-defense holster even more important. Concealed carry gun holsters should not move or relocate during everyday movements. It's important that a concealed holster stay in the same location throughout the day. That location is based on what you choose for your body and lifestyle, but it should remain consistent week after week, year after year.

The action of drawing and aiming should be a reflexive action that requires very little thought. The second that you put your hand toward your firearm to defend yourself but don't find it where you expect it, your brain and body will panic. The time you must spend searching, even if it's only a second or two, are very precious at a time when your life's in danger. This should hammer home the requirement to use a holster that stays in one place all the time. It must be there when you need it.

Slight shifts in movement can also cause skin irritation and make carrying uncomfortable. Regular concealed carry is not possible if it's annoying and painful. Snagging and sagging are the two biggest pieces of evidence that your concealed carry holster is not right for you. As you move throughout the day, your waistband, shirt, or jacket should never catch on any part of your holster or firearm.

A holster that sags below your waistline or weighs down your pants is not fit for you. Consider a stronger belt made for supporting a holstered handgun, pants that fit differently, or a small caliber firearm that weighs less.

If the holster moves from its original location even the slightest bit, a fast and effective draw is impossible. To make the problem worse, a holster that rubs your skin, damages your clothes, or weighs down your pants is annoying and uncomfortable. No matter how powerful the protection, a person is less likely to carry regularly if the concealed handgun is something that needs to be adjusted frequently.

When you don't carry concealed on a consistent basis, you lose any familiarity you've developed through practice and your ability to quickly find and use your handgun is diminished.

Here's how a concealed carry holster protects your firearm over time.

Exposure to dust and debris will ruin a concealed handgun. Even the smallest items can make a concealed carry handgun useless when it's needed the most. Over time of course, the overall condition of a gun will be eroded away without proper protection and regular cleaning.

Armed self-defense puts handguns through regular wear and tear during the day and regular practice at the firing range or dry fire practice at home can slowly put the parts and quality of the gun at risk.

If your preferred method of armed self-defense is off body or pocket carry, there are some specific things to be aware of. Small items like keys, paper clips, or coins will have a terrible effect on a concealed handgun.

Often found in pockets, purses, backpacks, and messenger bags, these innocent items cause scratches and leave behind debris that can quickly deteriorate the finish and function of a handgun. Not only do they damage a gun's components, they can cause serious malfunctions.

Setting aside the long term damage that these items can inflict over time, an item like a forgotten paper clip can cause a trigger pull and that mistake can cost a life.

Don't overlook the importance of a proper concealed carry gun holster. Take the time to consult with professionals about which style of holster is best for you. Attend gun safety and familiarization trainings to ensure that a small mistake in choosing a concealed carry holster doesn't have big consequences.

Methods of Concealed Carry

Inside the Waistband (IWB) Holster

For armed self-defense, many choose to go with a compact firearm secured in a holster that fits inside the waistband. These are the best option for concealment, as they can be easily covered by a shirt and leave an impression that's barely noticeable.

In these types of holster systems, the gun and holster are kept between your body and the waistline of your pants. Some choose to keep the holster between an undershirt and the waistline while an overshirt drapes over in order to conceal with the most comfort.

Belt Holster

These traditional holsters are probably what come to mind when you think of a handgun holster. They can be called Outside the Waistband (OWB) holsters as well. These holsters feature belt loops through which you put a sturdy belt made to support a holster and firearm. These types of holsters hold a firearm securely on the waist, leaving it visible without an overcoat or long baggy shirt.

Belt holsters are best for anyone who is frequently standing or moving on their feet for most of the day. They offer quick access to the firearm and a very secure method of retention throughout many different activities.

Anyone who finds themselves at a desk or in a car during the day might complain that a belt holster is uncomfortable. While holsters in

American Concealed

this style are sturdy and secure, they also don't offer much in the way of flexibility.

Depending on the size of the firearm you're carrying, they can dig into your hip or side if you're seated or moving into different positions. Carrying a firearm in this style is called "open carry." Laws concerning the practice vary widely from state to state. If this is how you choose to be armed for self-defense, take the time to research the laws and consider the implications of carrying in such a way that shows everyone that you're armed.

Paddle Holster

Holsters are also available in what's called a "Paddle" style, referring to the shape of the clip that secures the holster to the waist of your pants. It addresses some of the downsides of belt holsters, namely versatility and comfort.

Unlike a belt holster, the paddle holster does not rely on your belt for security. The paddle can fit comfortably on the waist of your pants without being restricted by belt loops. This type of holster adapts to your personal preferences as to the best carry location for you.

The Location of Your Concealed Handgun

Concealed weapons should not be visible to anyone. There are a few reasons for this. First, an exposed defensive handgun opens you up to negative opinions from anyone who sees the gun. No matter where you stand on the issue, it's one that divides people and stirs emotions.

Even when you have a gun for the best reasons, another person might see it and feel that you are putting people in danger. It isn't unheard of to read news stories about store customers calling police, notifying staff, or even tackling a person who has accidentally revealed their concealed handgun.

Second, exposing a concealed firearm increases the odds that someone may try to steal from you. It might sound illogical, but when you consider how expensive and desirable a nice handgun is, you can see why showing a gun is similar to showing people any other expensive item.

Lastly, showing off your handgun to your friends can turn from fun to danger very quickly. It's important to remember that even if your gun isn't seen, you can still alert others nearby that you're carrying by talking with others about it. Boasting about carrying and talking about what guns you have on your waist can attract attention that you do not want.

Even if you're just talking with your friends, you cannot know the intentions of people nearby. Having a gun on your waist does not make you invincible. Keep your discussions and gun handling to a time and place where you can be sure to be safe.

If a concealed carry holster and firearm becomes visible during any everyday movements it must be corrected. Normal actions like crouching or removing coats should never reveal a gun's location. Really, there can't be any excuses for accidentally revealing a concealed self-defense handgun.

With a little research, you can explore a wide variety of holster styles online and at your local gun shop. There are holster options to accommodate any lifestyle needs you may have.

Printing occurs when the outline of your concealed handgun can be seen through the material of your pants or through your shirt. This can be true for a pocket carry holster or when the impression of a holster on the waistline is seen through a t-shirt.

The correct holster you choose should leave a smooth impression on the outside of pants or bags that does not indicate a concealed firearm. If carrying on your waist, whether inside or outside the waistline, is important to you, choose clothing that adequately covers the holster system.

American Concealed

Pocket Carry

For some situations and lifestyles, pocket carry is a perfect option for armed self-defense. Pocket carry is a popular choice for individuals looking for full concealment within the pocket of pants or a jacket.

Those who practice pocket carry usually don't want a holster on their hip for fashion reasons or workplace requirements. With pocket carry, you won't need a larger shirt or vest to hang over your waistline.

Popular guns for pocket carry are usually smaller calibers like a .380, .25, or .22. There is debate among self-defense enthusiasts about the effectiveness of these calibers as opposed to larger ones, but the convenience of compact pistols is certainly appealing to many regardless of that.

We'll examine compact pistols a little more in a later chapter, but for now it helps to point out that those are the ideal handguns for pocket carry.

Here's what to look for in holsters for pocket carry.

Before getting into holsters for pocket carry, we should first mention that a pocket is not a holster. What do we mean by that? Well, simply sliding a gun into your pocket is never a good idea. Pocket carry without a holster can cause a host of problems. The correct pocket holster keeps debris and other objects from accidentally engaging the trigger or damaging the frame.

A holster will also keep the gun upright and in position for a fast draw. Without a holster, the gun will move around in your pocket, sometimes even managing to arrange itself with the muzzle pointed directly up at your face. A holster will help it stay in one place as you move throughout the day.

Using a holster has another advantage. It will stay in the pocket during your draw, not stay attached to the firearm. Drawing your gun to protect a threat to your life while also pulling out the holster would

Armed Self-Defense Handbook

put you in considerable danger. Pocket holsters feature construction and gripping fabrics that help it to firmly stay inside your pocket during your draw.

The correct holster will break up the outline of the handgun, increasing concealment and probably your comfort too. As we mentioned earlier, printing is a way of disclosing to people that you are carrying, and that sets you up for possible problems. A pocket holster is constructed to leave a smooth and plain impression to anyone who might casually see you.

How to draw your firearm from a pocket holster.

One advantage of pocket carry is the casual way you can access your firearm. Pocket carry offers full concealment for armed self-defense. Slowly taking your grip in preparation to draw brings less attention to yourself, should that be required in your situation.

Many find that side pockets allow for the best pocket carry drawing. The best way to draw your defensive firearm is to keep your hand as flat as possibly until the gun is fully drawn. As you enter your pocket, flatten your hand and place your index finger along the frame, not on the trigger.

Pull the gun straight up and out before bringing the sights to your target. Place your finger on the trigger only when you're clear of your pocket and you're sure that the target must be destroyed. Bring the gun up to a natural firing position, with your arms fully extended toward you target.

Regular practice is crucial for pocket carry. The best way to build your skills for drawing is to start small. With an unloaded firearm, first practice getting to your gun quickly and cleanly. When you're able to access your firearm in your pocket comfortably with your finger along the frame, move on to your draw and and sight alignment.

As you practice locating, drawing, and aiming your firearm

from your pocket, pay special attention to the security of the holster. The holster should stay in your pocket after your draw, and should be easy to locate for reholstering after firing.

While practicing drawing for pocket carry, be sure to wear the same clothes that you would normally wear while carrying concealed. The more your firing range practice simulates your everyday carry, the more prepared you'll be for a self-defense scenario.

While firing through your pocket is certainly possible in an emergency, it shouldn't be done unless the situation is dire. This strategy would work best through an outer garment like a coat, but should still be avoided if possible.

Firing your gun through your pants pocket puts your entire leg and foot in danger and, as we mentioned earlier, your finger shouldn't be on the gun's trigger until you are sighted on a target that must be destroyed.

When pocket carrying, always keep the holster and gun on your person. The smaller size of the gun and compact nature of the holster can increase the odds of accidentally leaving it somewhere your don't intend to, or moving around on your body. Discipline is crucial, and taking the gun from your pocket at any point throughout the day should be strictly avoided if at all possible.

Off Body Carry

So far, we've reviewed the various holsters available for concealed carry. As we said, there is a holster to match any body type and lifestyle out there. Sometimes, carrying concealed off of your body is what's necessary. You might carry a backup defensive firearm in a bag or you may find that a purse is the best place for you to keep your gun. Either way, there are some strict rules to follow to keep the firearm secured but also accessible.

Secure access to your firearms.

Choosing to carry off of your body means that your firearm can be accessed without your knowledge. It's necessary that you always keep your purse or bag close to you. The probability that you'll leave your firearm behind is a risk of off-body carry.

When a firearm is in your bag there may be the temptation to check on it and reassure yourself that the gun is there and secure. The more often that you check your bag, the higher the chances of an accidental discharge.

You probably have a purse or other bag that you use regularly. If at all possible, switch to a bag that is made specifically for off-body concealed carry. There are many options that feature secure zippers, sewn-in holsters, and hidden pockets sized specifically for your handgun. The ways that carrying your handgun haphazardly in a random pocket of your purse or messenger bag can go wrong are just too numerous.

The need to manage access by children and other unauthorized people is a high priority for off-body carry. Children know that purses and bags usually contain gum, candy, or interesting items like smartphones. A locking zipper and a sharp eye are required if children may have access to your bag.

Generally speaking, thieves know that bags contain something valuable. They don't always care exactly what's contained in the bag, but are more than willing to take their chances in the hope that they end up with something good. Make sure your bag has strong straps, stays close by your side or back, and has securely fitting latches or zippers.

Consistency is the key for off body carry. The more often you carry, the better your ability to protect yourself. You'll find and draw your weapon faster and you'll grow more confident each and every time you carry.

Carrying occasionally sets you up for mistakes because you haven't developed the habit. You'll need to think before finding your gun and

American Concealed

the idea that you're armed will be at the forefront of your mind all day.

It's imperative that you bring your off body carry bag with you to the range. Just as you'd practice drawing and firing from your holster if you were carrying on your hip or shoulder, you must practice accessing and using your firearm from your bag. Try to simulate how you would be holding or opening the bag at various points during the day and practice those movements at the range.

Don't feel embarrassed about pulling your defensive weapon out of a backpack, purse, or messenger bag at the range. The firing range can be an intimidating place, and for that reason many people avoid going. They don't want to seem like they don't know what they're doing and are afraid of making a mistake.

If off body carry is what works best for you, you also know what type of practice you need to improve your accuracy and speed. Gun owners are largely a very friendly group and are very willing to talk about concealed carry. If you have a question, don't hesitate to ask the range manager.

Carrying a Backup CCW

Carrying concealed means being prepared for anything, even if that means reacting to the loss or malfunction of your primary concealed handgun. During a situation in which you feel your life is threatened by an attacker or group of attackers, it's possible that your firearm may malfunction or you may run out of ammunition.

At this point you would need to resort to either your physical combat skills or a second weapon. It's a scenario none of us want to imagine, but we must prepare for it nonetheless. For some, there's no question about carrying a second firearm for just such a scenario. Contrary to some opinions, carrying a backup piece doesn't necessarily mean you're taking armed self-defense over the top.

There are equal numbers who disagree about where to carry, what caliber to carry, and a long list of other issues. When it comes down to it, if a backup defensive handgun is what you need to stay safe, then it's a good idea. Just as with any other aspect of concealed carry, it's up to you to decide what systems and strategies work best for you. With the right model and placement, adding a backup can be an easy transition. Here are some reasons to consider it.

You're unable to retain your primary weapon because of an injury or altercation.

A self-defense scenario is very different from your target practice at the range. These altercations happen very quickly and injuries frequently occur. You might be taken to the ground in a fight or lose your grip on your weapon due to an injury.

Earlier in the book, we discussed the importance of keeping your gun concealed and not showing it off to others. This becomes important in a scenario where you'll need to defend yourself. If your attacker knows about your gun, they might try to take it from you during the altercation or injure you so that you can't access it.

Your primary weapon malfunctions.

In the heat of a violent struggle clearing a malfunction might not be an option. An attacker won't stop and wait while you correct the malfunction and take aim again. A fresh backup weapon can be on hand quickly.

With practice and proper placement, it can be faster than reloading.

Carrying a backup magazine is pretty standard, and with practice you may even get pretty fast at reloading your spare. In fact, carrying a spare magazine is a good first step in the process toward a backup handgun.

American Concealed

An extra magazine or two would be a great asset if you were really in need of extra ammo. In states where the magazine capacity is lower than 10, many people armed for self-defense feel that an extra magazine is necessary.

A violent attack will rarely require you to empty a magazine, but scenarios that have multiple attackers or take place in an outdoor area can mean multiple shots. If you feel that an attack from a larger group of people is something that could happen to you, you might want to consider carrying an easily accessible backup.

If you carry a backup, make it a serious commitment.

Carry one weapon first until you've become proficient at drawing, firing, and reloading. After you've spent time practicing and carrying one handgun regularly, slowly get comfortable with carrying additional magazines or non-lethal weapons like pepper spray.

When having these everyday carry items with you is no longer stressful or uncomfortable, you might consider carrying a backup gun. Adding another firearm to your daily carry takes time and expertise to manage responsibly. You'll need to think through your decision carefully, since you'll be shouldering double the responsibility every time you're out.

Carry both concealed weapons regularly. This requires a commitment to safe carrying, and should only be done by those who have experience carrying, dealing with malfunctions, and self-defense situations. If you're making the commitment to carrying a backup, stick with it. Your mind and body will slowly get accustomed to carrying two weapons and soon accessing them will be second nature.

Tactical Gear for Concealed Carry

There's no shortage of gear and accessories when it comes to firearms and concealed carry. First and foremost, get comfortable with carrying your firearm and only add new gear after you've determined a need and practiced using new items consistently.

Spare Ammunition Holders

Sometimes, people who are armed for self-defense choose to carry a spare magazine of ammunition. This allows you to have access to even more ammunition than is in your concealed carry pistol, giving you even more opportunities to defend yourself.

There are two great reasons to carry a spare magazine. One, if you and any others you might be with are threatened by a large group, more shots may be required to successfully defend yourself. In this case, you wouldn't want to be caught with less ammunition than there are attackers.

Two, you should practice safe handling through all types of malfunctions during your practice at the firing range, but in the heat of the moment it can be nearly impossible. It's usually just faster to clear the malfunction, release the magazine, and use your spare magazine to continue your self-defense.

Carrying a concealed handgun already requires extra effort and responsibility, so adding in a spare magazine can weigh heavily on a new concealed carrier. First, get comfortable carrying concealed on a daily basis, then consider adding a spare magazine to your daily routine. Carrying a spare magazine of ammunition with you everywhere you go certainly is not a requirement of armed self-defense.

If you carry regularly and you feel that you'd be better off with more ammunition, go for it. It can be uncomfortable in certain situations, but there are some easy guidelines to follow to be sure that you maximize your comfort and safety.

American Concealed

Suppressors

There are some very good reasons for adding a suppressor to your handgun training. They're easier to purchase than you think, and they're now legal in 40 states. In order to add a suppressor, you'll first need to get the real facts on what they really do. That means forgetting pretty much everything you've seen in movies and video games.

Despite sometimes being called silencers, they don't totally silence gun shots. And they're perfectly legal in many states and available for use by any gun owner who is willing to go through the effort to obtain one.

In 2015 Minnesota became the 40th state to legalize handgun suppressors. Despite the usual arguments that they put law enforcement and bystanders at increased risk, legislation in favor of suppressor sales has significant support in many states.

The use of suppressors opens up new avenues for guns store sales and makes target shooting easier to enjoy. Both are benefits to the local community and economy.

A suppressor will lower the sound of gunfire to a less damaging level, which is one of the main benefits. A suppressor can lower the decibels of a shot by 20-30, making firing easier and more comfortable. Long-time shooters can have reduced hearing loss and neighborhood firing ranges can comply with noise regulations.

The reduced noise and muzzle flash can also improve accuracy for beginner shooters as well, allowing them to fire more calmly and ease fear of a loud blast.

The extensive background check process and high overall cost of purchasing a suppressor goes a long way to reduce any criminal use. The entire process can run up to nine months to a year in most cases. Suppressors are categorized as firearms by the federal government, resulting in a lengthy approval process.

To purchase one, you'll need to fulfill the application requirements of the Bureau of Alcohol, Tobacco, Firearms and Explosives (ATF) and pay a tax fee. This "tax stamp" goes to the federal government instead of your state. Suppressors are available online and in reputable gun shops. Do your research beforehand to be sure you're following the correct procedures.

You may also want to register the suppressor to a corporation or a gun trust, thus saving you some steps. For the best advice, always talk with a trustworthy lawyer about your options.

Laser Sights

Handgun owners are always looking for ways to improve accuracy and reliability. When personal safety is at risk, a handgun needs to be as effective as possible with very little room for error. A handgun equipped with a laser sight is an option that many are choosing for cost effectiveness and other benefits. This type of sight can be effective in many situations.

When is a laser sight most effective?

Many of the incidents that would require a handgun owner to use a gun for personal protection occur at night or in a building or home. These conditions are not ideal for handgun use.

Low light and confined spaces constrict movement and slow down mental decision making. A laser sight is designed specifically for these types of situations. A laser dot is best seen in low light environments.

In tight spaces such as hallways or bedrooms, a free range of arm movement may not be an option. The laser sight removes the need for proper body stance and grip in small spaces and allows the user to quickly find the target.

American Concealed

How to use laser sights and self-defense.

Military and police professionals are well trained in managing stressful situations and combat scenarios. A person who keeps a handgun for personal protection may not have received such training and will feel the effects of stress and emotion much more when the decision to use a weapon is necessary.

In times of stress and panic, the gun's sights are often ignored. The target gets all of the attention. For this reason, many initial shots fired in self-defense are poorly aimed. This decreases the protective potential of the firearm.

Stressful and emotional situations may involve either multiple threats or bystanders who are involuntarily involved in the situation. A red dot sighted on a threat not only lets the target know for sure that a gun is trained on them, but it alerts bystanders that a firearm could be potentially used.

Laser sights do have some limitations.

There are some downfalls to the use of laser sights to be considered before adding them to your arsenal. They aren't for everyone, and using one without the proper training can be a real mistake. There are specific situations that could benefit from the use of a laser sight.

Situations with high light levels bring down the effective range of the laser sight down to as little as a few feet, and that can have a powerful effect on accuracy. When considering the addition of a laser sight, first think about the light levels of the environments in which you frequently find yourself. If the lighting and visibility of your home or work settings make navigating them dangerous, a laser sight could pay big benefits.

On the other hand, if you're able to stay indoors and don't move around much at night, a laser sight might not be worth the extra money and effort.

Another issue to consider is that with increased use of a laser sight, the user may come to rely on it instead of the traditional iron sights. It is important to note that a laser sight is an accommodation to the handgun and not a suitable substitute for the iron sights in some situations. It's essential that you invest the time into training with your traditional iron sights.

A laser sight is meant only as an addition to be used in the right circumstances. The practice you put in firing with your gun's iron sights will translate into faster and more accurate firing when the time comes. The benefits are numerous and have the potential to save lives.

Anyone choosing to employ the laser sight should take into account the environments in which it will be used as well as the training and practice necessary for correct use. Relying on laser sights when iron sights will do or using a laser sight in an outdoor sunlit area can have negative consequences.

Mounted Lights

When it comes to your defensive firearm, you want to make it work perfectly for you. You can take your concealed carry handgun to the next level with a mounted tactical light. When they're used correctly, a mounted light can have many benefits. There are some important elements to know about mounted lights before you start using them.

What are the benefits of a gun-mounted light?

Lights attached to the mounting rail of a handgun can help to identify a target without needing a separate hand. Simply identifying an aggressor can sometimes be enough of a deterrent to stop a violent incident.

An attacker that's attempting to use the darkness as cover may find that being visible takes away their advantage. With the distance that a quality mounted light shines, you give yourself a good amount of distance and time with which to work.

You can disable an attacker's vision and identify their weapons (or lack thereof) with a mounted light. Darkness can play to your attacker's advantage, but sudden bright lights in these cases can be enough to disable them temporarily. The power that some mounted lights throw off can be downright painful when it hits eyes unexpectedly.

A weapon-mounted light does not take the place of a flashlight, however. If you frequently find yourself in low light areas due to work or other reasons, you should consider adding a light to your concealed carry handgun.

Here's what to look for in a mounted tactical flashlight.

When selecting a light to mount on your handgun, first be sure it fits in your concealed carry holster, or purchase a holster that will accommodate the light. The online marketplace can be a great place to find products, but a mounted light for your defensive handgun really should be purchased by a reputable seller that allows you to first be sure it fits appropriately.

Be sure that the battery power source is high-quality and the on-off switch isn't too easily activated. This prevents accidental activation which can run down your battery life and make drawing unpredictable. Adding a mounted light means that you'll need to start including its maintenance along with the upkeep of your firearm, ammunition, and other gear.

Your life is possibly linked to the performance of this light, so check its functionality frequently and be sure the switches are tight and working properly. Clean the light's lens after use. Dirt and powder residue can blur the lens and make it less effective.

A proper mounted weapon light should be at least 100 lumens, and more for outdoor use. LED lights are brighter and more durable than incandescent varieties. Put this number in your research and take the time to choose wisely.

Consider the types of situations you're likely to find yourself in and what power of bulb you'll be needing. Outdoor darkness is quite a bit more expansive and usually requires more power, while your light goes farther on less in tighter indoor spaces.

How should you draw and shoot with a mounted light?

You must know these rules before carrying a firearm with a mounted tactical light.

First and foremost, a mounted light is not an illumination device. That means that it should never be used for anything other than firing at a target. Don't use a mounted light to search for your keys, when the power goes out at home, or to find the zipper in your tent. It's not a loaded flashlight, it's a gun with a light attached.

Put thought into what type of switch you'll want to use. Accidental discharges can happen when the shooter's finger slips or misses a light switch near the trigger guard. The best tactical lights feature switches forward of the trigger.

Look for lights with tail-cap switches or a button on the rail, as they keep your finger away from the trigger. Toggle switches should be fully ambidextrous, so that no matter what hand you use, the up-down movements have the same result.

Use lights that give you the option to toggle between momentary and constant on modes. You want to be able to easily change modes because self-defense situations can escalate rapidly.

Practice frequently. If you carry concealed and decide to add a mounted light, you'll need to work on your draw and switch activation. Even adding a small addition to your standard firearm can change your movements.

Don't use improvised devices to attach your tactical light. Things like Velcro, clamps, or adhesives are not as trustworthy as a proper mounting. You'll also want to choose an option that allows you to easily attach or remove for maintenance.

Using Hollow Point Ammunition for Self-Defense

Hollow point ammunition has some distinct features that set it apart from its round nose, full metal jacket counterparts. The search for ammunition that will serve you best will bring you plenty of options. Every handgun owner should take the time to research and practice with all types of ammunition to decide which works best and fits their specific needs. Considering the advantages and disadvantages of hollow point ammunition will give gun owners the knowledge to make the correct choice.

What makes hollow point ammunition unique?

A deep dimple in the nose of the bullet is the best known and easily recognizable feature of hollow point bullets. These bullets are designed to expand on contact with the target, thus creating a larger hole and increasing the stopping power of the firearm. When seen in comparison to a round nose or ball ammunition, the differences are easy to see.

Hollow points have some distinct advantages.

When it comes to self-defense, a handgun loaded with hollow point bullets has a few advantages over one loaded with full metal jacket or round nosed lead bullets. When an attacker is in full force, the stopping power of your ammunition is especially important. Hollow points expand, much like an umbrella, upon contact.

This means an increase in the force it delivers when the bullet hits its mark. In this way, hollow point bullets are a way to increase this "knock down power" in handguns of a smaller caliber.

Can one type of bullet really be considered safer than others?

In the case of hollow points, yes. The rounded and smooth surface of full metal jacket rounds means that these bullets are more likely to pass through the target. In this case, rounds intended to stop an attacker could travel through the body and result in less initial damage.

These wayward rounds can also keep traveling, through either a body or wall, and make contact with innocent bystanders. The expanding capability of the hollow point decreases the likelihood of this scenario, thus keeping bystanders more safe.

Hollow points also have a few down sides.

As with all types of ammunition, there are some disadvantages to weigh. Hollow point ammunition is more expensive than round nose, and that makes practice pricey. Handgun owners should practice regularly with the gun and ammo that will be used in self-defense scenarios, and in this case the cost could add up.

For general target practice, round nose options are a much better option, for both reliability and cost.

The debate over placement versus caliber continues to be a topic for handgun owners. Some argue that a well-placed bullet, no matter what the caliber, can be more effective. Others are confident that a larger caliber bullet means a deadlier option.

Some will argue that using hollow points is pointless when a larger caliber like a .45 ACP or .357 Magnum carries all the stopping power necessary to bring down an attacker in close proximity.

Weigh Your Ammo Options Carefully.

Handgun owners looking for the most effective ammunition for personal protection should consider loading up with hollow points. Hollow points are an excellent option for home self-defense because they are less likely to pass through the target or walls and put family in danger.

Hollow point bullets also mean that fewer rounds may be required to bring down an assailant, and that means better outcomes for all involved. For the best results in self-defense with a handgun, consider using hollow point ammunition.

How to Choose a Caliber for Concealed Carry

There's a myth about people who carry concealed. People think that they're all carrying hefty .45 and booming .357 revolvers, thinking they're John Wayne or Dirty Harry.

The truth is far different. Concealed carry permits and purchases are expanding all across the country. Not surprisingly, the popularity of small-caliber handguns is also on the rise. Many people prefer to carry "mouse guns" that chamber smaller rounds like .380 ACP or a .22 LR.

Smaller caliber guns are fun to shoot.

Training and regular practice is the best way to be effective. When a gun is easy to shoot, practice is more likely. Long-time shooters may claim that concealed carry isn't about fun, it's about powerful self-defense. They're not wrong, but a big gun fired by the wrong type of person could discourage them from wanting to carry right from the start. Women and young folks also find them easy to manage and fire.

Taking the family to the range for target shooting and basic education is fun and easy with a smaller caliber pistol. Choosing a smaller caliber piece for armed self-defense can help to ease stress because the carrier knows they'll be able to handle it effectively.

Smaller handguns are easy to carry.

Concealment is easy with compact handguns. There's no need to wear baggy clothes and pocket carry is a convenient option. They're a great option for the office or for individuals who have problems with mobility and dexterity. For whatever reason, there are some in the concealed carry community who feel that carrying a handgun should be uncomfortable. They feel that the weight and pain is part of the responsibility of owning a firearm.

Carrying every single day certainly is part of the lifestyle. But if a large-caliber gun is burdensome for you, chances are you'll end up leaving it at home. Armed self-defense shouldn't prevent you from being able to complete your daily activities.

It's about being ready in the event of the absolute worst case scenario, and you shouldn't feel compelled to carry a gun that's far too large to be reasonable for your circumstances.

"Mouse guns" are more than strong enough for self-defense.

There's an ongoing debate over just how effective each caliber is for armed self-defense. It really boils down to personal preference, since everyone has a preference for the power they're comfortable firing.

A person accurately firing a .22 is more effective than someone wielding a .45 firearm that isn't right for them. No matter the size, a gun is your best option for deterring and eliminating a threat to your life. Ultimately, the caliber you carry is up to personal preference. Carrying a certain caliber just because someone else does or because a gun is popular could be a mistake.

Carry what's comfortable and what fits your lifestyle best. Carry a caliber that allows you to practice regularly.

Carrying Concealed in Warm Weather

When your thermometer rises, so does your temper. Research is now showing that extreme weather results in increases in crime and violence. In fact, a recent *New York Times* article compared the results of 27 research studies on weather and violence and found that all over the world, extreme weather almost always results in more conflict between groups and violence between individuals.

Areas affected by drought and long periods of high temperatures will almost surely result in more fights, attacks, robberies, and erratic behaviors. Prepare to protect yourself this summer by carrying a concealed handgun. There are ways to do it while wearing shorts and t-shirts, and you can do it very comfortably.

Comfort and concealment are the two most important things to consider when carrying in warm weather. Most guys will be wearing t-shirts, polos, or a short sleeve button-down during these warmer months. Ladies will probably choose smaller tops and maybe skirts to keep cool.

There are holsters and methods of carrying that fit any clothing choice, just be sure to choose correctly based on what you're wearing. Inside the Waistband (IWB) holsters are a less revealing option and fit nicely under a t-shirt and pants.

These holsters keep the handgun inside, rather than allowing the gun to bulge out along the waistline. Choose a smaller more compact weapon because a larger model may dig into your torso or leg.

Pocket carry is a great option if you're wearing shorts or if you'll be moving frequently. Remember to always use a pocket carry holster. Never just slide a gun into your pocket. Foreign objects can damage the gun and interfere with your draw. Items like a pen or keys can easily manipulate the trigger without your knowledge. A pocket holster covers the trigger guard to prevent these types of accidents.

A pocket holster also holds the weapon upright in your pocket. When you draw your weapon your grip is correct. Choose a pocket holster that is made to stay in your pocket upon drawing. Material like "alligator skin" is designed to catch on the other material so that only your weapon is removed from your pocket.

A "belly band" style holster is made of elastic and attaches with velcro. It contains several pouches and areas designed to carry a handgun and other items like a pocket knife or money. These holsters are not meant for speed, as you will need to lift your shirt to access the weapon.

Compression clothing for concealed carry is also an option for men and women in the summer months. You can find a variety of tight-fitting shirts and undershorts that are modified to hold a concealed handgun.

They are perfect for summer weather because they fit closely to the body or ride low on the hips. If your clothing is slimming or doesn't have pockets, this type of holster is a good option.

Concealed Carry in Cold Weather

You may be tempted to think that concealed carry is much easier in the colder months. It's partly true, all of those layers do conceal a defensive handgun quite well. But they also make it more difficult to access and use that weapon in self-defense. Fortunately, with a little planning and practice you can carry concealed in the winter without problems.

First, consider how all of that extra clothing and accessories meant to keep you warm can actually make self-defense more difficult. Hats pulled down over your eyes and hands stuffed into pockets can lower your awareness of your surroundings and make you more vulnerable to attack. Your winter clothing should keep you warm while also allowing freedom of movement and good visibility.

If the weather calls for hand protection, you should consider wearing gloves that fit closely to the fingers and feature a pad on the shooting finger. The material must give you a solid grip on the handgun and not interfere with the shot.

For a holster, keep a few rules in mind. First, stay as consistent as possible with what you'd carry in the warmer parts of the year. If you've been carrying concealed every day (and you should be), you're already familiar with the location of your concealed handgun.

American Concealed

Drastically changing its location might force you to think twice when a situation demands speed. You have other holstering options to consider, so maintain similarity in terms of the firearm and the side of your body at the very least.

Despite falling slightly out of favor among those who carry concealed, shoulder holster systems can actually offer some benefits for cold weather carry. Normally considered too bulky for the majority of situations and clothing styles, shoulder holsters can be an excellent method of carry in winter months because they are easy to conceal and access while wearing an overcoat.

The popularity of smaller caliber handguns for concealed carry has made pocket holsters a common method of concealment. In colder weather, we often cover our upper body much more than our legs. This makes accessing pocket holsters easier than unbuttoning and moving a coat aside to access a hip or shoulder system.

No matter what choice you make for holstering your handgun, there's one aspect of cold weather carry that can't be overlooked. Practicing your draw and shot outside in cold weather is simply the best way to be sure that you'll react quickly and efficiently in an outdoor self-defense situation.

The frigid temperatures, snow, rain, and ice that accompany the winter months often discourage gun owners from getting out to practice as much as they would in the spring and summer. Regular practice keeps your skills sharp and your mind ready, and the winter is no time for taking a break.

Going through the motions of accessing your concealed handgun, drawing, and firing is the only way to discover any gaps in your knowledge or obstacles to your defense. You'll need to work with chilly fingers and toes, as well as moving through layers of clothing and outerwear.

Concealed Carry in the Workplace

Maybe you're working late and you're the last one out of the office. Pulling an early shift that means you're unlocking the doors in the early morning hours? If there is any risk of being attacked or your job puts you into risky situations, you might consider carrying concealed.

Carrying concealed in the office workplace presents some challenges. In most workplaces, employees must follow a business casual dress code, and this style is not always conducive to concealed carry.

Keeping your handgun concealed is always a requirement, but concealment at work is even more important. There may be consequences related to your employment, frightened and uninformed co-workers, and even your paycheck.

Consider a small caliber for better concealment.

A smaller pistol or revolver that is easy to conceal may be your best option for office carry. A smaller handgun like a .380 Colt Mustang or Ruger LC9 offer a very low profile but pack the power and reliability you need.

There are some very good options for holsters and off-body carry at work. If your workplace has a strict dress code, you'll need to do some extra work to find a holster that fits your needs. An Inside the Waistband holster is a good option if you wear a suit jacket or care to place the firearm between your undershirt and button-up.

A pocket holster or ankle holster are also options to test. These would depend largely on the movements that you do while at work and what type of pants are permitted.

Easy accessibility is an element that must be balanced with concealment. If an on-the-body holster doesn't seem like an option for your workplace, consider carrying in a bag, briefcase, or planner that accommodates a firearm.

American Concealed

How should you handle the issue with your employer?

After you've reviewed your state's laws concerning carry in places of business and after you've read over your workplace handbook for references to the same, you'll need to decide how to bring the issue up with your employer or coworkers.

Every situation is different. On one side, never disclosing means you won't be told you can't carry, but it also means that if someone sees your gun or you use it, it could cause a serious issue in the office. Despite your responsible use and regular practice, your co-workers and supervisor may hold strong feelings about spending every day in such close proximity to a deadly weapon.

On the other hand, disclosing to your employer that you carry concealed could open a good dialogue about the issue and they may be willing to permit it. The best tactic is to be respectful and knowledgeable prior to the discussion. Know your rights, the state laws, and your options for responsible carry before you start the discussion.

Concealed carry in the workplace is dependent on many factors. Do your research and weigh your options. Be prepared to have a dialogue about the issue with colleagues and supervisors. There is no substitute for being understanding and respectful, and in the end that may be the reason you're permitted to carry.

Concealed Carry in the Classroom

These days, teachers are doing more than just teaching the ABCs. They're now responsible for the safety of their students and themselves. Three states are considering whether concealed carry is the best way to keep schools safe.

Several state governments in are currently considering bills that would allow concealed carry in K-12 schools. A teacher's ability to carry a concealed handgun in the school classroom varies from state to state.

Some must register with the school board, while other states like Utah (as of 2014) do not require the teacher to tell anyone. If someone should consider attacking a Utah school, they'll enter not knowing who may be armed and ready to defend themselves and students with lethal force.

Among the arguments against concealed carry in schools, the fear that students are actually in more danger stands tallest. Some parents and teacher groups argue that if a concealed handgun is accidentally discovered or fired, it's the students that could suffer.

In 2014, a Utah teacher accidentally discharged her concealed handgun in the bathroom before the start of the school day. There were no lethal injuries and no teachers or students nearby, but news reports of the incident rose questions among parents' groups about safety concerns. There are strong arguments in favor of arming our nation's teachers.

Rural communities are in danger when you consider the fact that most active shooter situations in schools are over in 10 minutes or less (according to Los Angeles County Sheriff's Department statistics). This puts them at a loss as they wait on a law enforcement response.

Without a concealed firearm, the tactics and weapons that teachers are taught to use against an active shooter are questionable. Some teachers are advised to use random classroom items like scissors, backpacks stuffed with books, chairs, or belts in defense against a killer determined to take the lives of children with a gun. The thought of a teacher swinging a belt or throwing a stapler at a killer with a gun is enough to give one pause.

Significant budget cuts at the state and local level can leave schools scrambling for security coverage. Reports from the U.S. Department of Education show that layoffs of counselors, decreases in sports and afterschool programming, and lack of security personnel all combine to increase the danger of incidents.

American Concealed

Ultimately, it's up to elected state lawmakers to decide how teachers can best protect their students if an active shooter situation arises. Teachers that do decide to carry concealed handguns to school will be most effective if they undergo certification and tactical training that prepares them for protecting students in an active shooter situation.

Concealed Carry on Campus

The political climate today is one in which every person is deserving of a voice. Because of where they live and study, college students frequently find that armed self-defense is not an option for them. The policies of many colleges and universities require students living on and off campus to leave their legally acquired handguns at home or locked in their cars in the parking lot.

Sadly, this regulation is often in place under the guise of "increasing student safety." Many who argue for its implementation also use the reasoning that college students (even those that have legally obtained a permit and firearm) are somehow incapable of using a gun appropriately.

Dismissing college students as bumbling idiots incapable of any responsibility could end up costing lives. Making the argument that college students don't deserve to lawfully arm themselves puts them in serious danger.

Our American society is known worldwide for making sure that everyone has a free shot at success and appreciation, but in the case of campus carry we are surely dropping the ball.

Here are four good reasons why college students across the country should be allowed to carry, and ignoring them could result in disaster on campus.

College campuses are targets for violence.

There have been a number of well-documented violent attacks

involving an active shooter on college campuses in the past few years. The crowded spaces filled with busy, preoccupied students offer deranged individuals a target-rich environment. Criminals and unstable individuals may have the knowledge that students in these areas are not permitted to carry a firearm for self-defense.

They may use that to their advantage. Can we ever know exactly if this is a strategy used by violent perpetrators? Probably not. But, the very chance that this idea could pass through a shooter's mind should be enough to change the regulation.

These incidents get news exposure, but far more violence occurs on university campuses that is swept under the rug in order to keep up the polished image of many schools. Violent acts like rape and physical assault are on the rise as student populations grow.

A school's reputation is crucial to its ability to grow, and every school wants that. Violence on campus is a huge deterrent to new student enrollment, so smaller, less newsworthy incidents are frequently handled using campus security and school-based punishments. This means the true number of violent acts rarely reaches the news media, much to the appreciation of the school's top levels.

Colleges are filled with responsible, law-abiding citizens.

More often than not, students come from the local community and are taking classes part-time. Colleges and universities are no longer made up of only young people fresh from home. In a recent violent event at a community college in Oregon, more part-time students attended than full-time. This ratio reflects a growing trend in this country, and illustrates that many campuses are now public grounds serving a wide range of people.

Non-traditional students are tax-paying citizens who obey the law, and they deserve the right to protect themselves by carrying concealed. Assuming that every student on campus is just there to party is totally off target.

Visit any smaller campus in the nation and you'll find few security guards and even fewer of them that are armed with anything more than pepper spray and a flashlight.

Classes include instruction in self-defense and constitutional rights.

There's no better environment for delivering instruction about basic self-defense than a university. When students enroll for college classes they are given the opportunity to learn about how the constitution enables them to lawfully protect themselves. Classes in a variety of disciplines deliver instruction in community participation and civic responsibility.

Students are already on campus to learn and get experience in different lines of work and culture. They're eager to learn how they can bring positive changes to society, and concealed carry instruction increases safety across the board.

There is just as much stress off campus as there is on campus.

A common argument against campus carry is that college students are under too much stress to safely carry a firearm. Opponents say students are so worried about upcoming tests or roommate troubles that they couldn't possibly arm themselves for self-defense.

Would they then say that life outside of college is so relaxing? Opponents of campus carry need to face the facts and realize that anyone living and working out in the community deals with just as much stress, maybe even more, than a college student. Millions of certified and trained citizens are able to carry concealed without issue, even while handling car payments, mortgages, taking the kids to school, and high-pressure careers.

It's time to stop assuming that all university students are immature party animals that don't deserve to protect themselves when a violent criminal walks onto campus intending to cause destruction.

Many students are there to work hard, often after already putting in a shift on the job elsewhere. Treat college students with the same respect you'd give anyone else living in your community, and make armed self-defense a reality for them.

Part Three

Fundamentals of Defensive Shooting

American Concealed

Self-defense incidents most commonly occur in low light settings and victims usually have very little time to react. Surviving these critical scenarios requires automatic defensive responses that quickly de-escalate the situation.

Preparing for self-defense is a continuous process. Proper shooting technique takes regular practice to learn and maintain. It requires a strong knowledge of the laws that apply to you when you feel threatened. The best strategy is to inform yourself of current issues and prepare yourself before you even holster your weapon.

There is no need to live your life living in fear of what threats might be hiding around every corner. The best way to alleviate fear is to be prepared for a variety of situations. Proper preparation leads to confidence, and confidence allows you to enjoy all that life has to offer.

Just as we reinforced earlier, the best strategy is to first build a solid foundation of basic skills. When they've been mastered, you can then build upon them and add more sophisticated tactics. Seasoned shooters with plenty of experience still spend time practicing fundamental gun-handling skills.

Defensive shooting is fundamentally much different than other types of shooting like hunting or target shooting. Unlike these two types, defensive shooting means that you think that your life is in immediate danger. Other less permanent types of self-defense are not available to you and you must use your concealed weapon to critically injure an immediate threat.

Hours of practice repeating the same movements may not seem like your idea of a good time. In fact, if practicing and responsibility isn't really your thing, concealed carry is probably not for you anyway. The reason for the practice becomes apparent when the time to defend yourself arrives.

It may be in the car, on an evening stroll with a friend, or at a busy shopping mall. Preparing yourself for defending your life and the lives of others is a vital practice.

Defensive Body Positions

Target practice is an essential part of concealed carry, but you need to get out of your comfort zone if you want to really improve. When it comes down to it, target practice and real self-defense are very different situations.

The body positions for defensive shooting are not meant to be comfortable or deliver precision accuracy. They are meant to get the job done. Keep in mind that your main goal is to stay alive, so don't be afraid to get a little dirty and move around.

These are best practiced at an outdoor range. Be sure that it's safe to move closer to your target to better simulate a close self-defense encounter.

One and Two Leg Kneeling

To practice firing from the kneeling position, first draw your firearm and place your dominant-side knee down. Hold your head, shoulders, and arms squarely facing the target.

Before firing, be sure that you are in a position to easily transition to standing or walking forward or backward. Use your support hand to steady yourself as you move. If you're on two knees, first bring your support-side leg forward, then move your other foot to rise.

When you've tried your stances and can move between them easily, begin adding firing to the process.

Firing While on Your Back

If you've somehow fallen or tripped and you end up on your back, you need to be able to fire accurately. First lower yourself to the ground and lay back, bring your head up off of the ground. Be sure to keep your legs spread and your knees bent, otherwise you risk shooting your toes instead of your target.

Square your shoulders and fully extend your arms, using a solid grip. Using as much strength as you have in your stomach muscles, bring your head and shoulders up to sight in as best you can. After you've practiced getting into position and then sitting up to rest, incorporate live fire into your practice.

If you find yourself on your back, it's likely that the situation is life or death. As you practice at the range, try to remain calm, breathe regularly, and use trigger discipline even though the strange position feels uncomfortable.

There are some additional things to remember for defensive firing.

Firing from defensive positions won't earn you perfect groups or headshots. They also can't be done for more than a few minutes at a time. If you've been attacked and you trip or are forced into an awkward position, you need to be able to defend yourself effectively and eliminate the threat.

Take the time to practice getting into position and then resting. Only then should you begin the process of drawing and reloading. When you feel that you're able to fire safely, begin adding live fire into your practice.

Gun Grip in Defensive Firing

Few things affect your shooting accuracy more than your grip. It's important that you hold the gun correctly from the time you draw, fire, reload, and holster again. Your grip is important if you engage in physical combat as well. A strong grip will help you retain your firearm and a steady aim throughout the conflict.

Overall, a good grip on the gun results in a natural sighting on your target. When your hands are holding the gun properly, you will find that they are trained on your target at least well enough to allow for somewhat accurate shooting.

A proper grip will also improve tracking, or the gun's return to its original position after each shot. A strong grip is flexible enough to absorb the recoil, or kick, of the gun after firing, but is firm enough to return your gun to its original position quickly, allowing for follow-up shots.

You should consider your thumb placement. For the best shooting grip, all parts of your hands, wrist, and arms must work together. Your thumbs are one of the toughest parts to master, so let's cover them first. It's important that the thumbs don't get in the way of the slide or controls, but that they stay in a position that allows you to still maintain control.

Thumb-Over-Thumb Technique

For beginning shooters, this technique is quick and easy to learn. It can be used on every type of handgun, regardless of size. The thumb of your dominant hand is placed overtop of the thumb on your non-dominant hand. This technique is fast and doesn't take much thought, making it appropriate for beginning shooters.

This grip can increase the tendency to hold the gun too tightly, though. The position of your thumbs can be close to the gun's safety, which is positive when releasing it purposely, but can be a problem if you are not prepared to fire. This is cause to remain very focused on the target and your decision to fire or not.

Thumbs Forward Technique

A more advanced grip popular with target shooters, called thumbs forward or straight thumbs, helps to increase accuracy and bring the hands and thumbs more flush with the gun itself. The non-dominant hand wraps around the dominant hand and fingers, nearly touching the

American Concealed

knuckles. The non-dominant thumb rests forward on the frame of the gun, while the other thumb rests just behind the top knuckle.

This grip helps one of the ultimate goals of sighting, which is to naturally train the hands to find the target. Aligning the thumbs helps to streamline the grip and bring the eyes and shoulders along for the ride.

Setting the wrist is very important to accuracy.

When both hands are exerting equal force on the grip of the gun, the importance of the wrist really comes into play. Tilting your wrist either up or down has drastic effects on accuracy and overall comfort when shooting. Hold your wrist firm and straight, putting pressure on the backstrap of the pistol.

A wrist that's solid and straight will prevent the hand from absorbing too much influence from the recoil. The left-to-right movements contained in the wrist must also be controlled to increase accuracy. A perfectly aligned wrist will be naturally trained toward the target throughout the firing and sighting process.

Apply correct pressure for optimum control.

Use the correct amount of force when gripping your handgun. There's no need to put the gun in a death grip. Maintain a comfortable amount of pressure. Gripping your handgun too tightly can put too much stress on your hand muscles and cause you to get tired quickly. If your grip is too loose your gun will not be steady and accuracy will decrease from shot to shot.

Trigger Squeeze

When you start analyzing your trigger squeeze you'll find that it's much more complicated than you think. Without a smooth and calculated trigger pull you'll find your accuracy and speed will suffer. In a violent

self-defense situation, accuracy and speed might be all you have.
Your trigger squeeze has a big impact on your accuracy.

When you're about to pull the trigger, place the tip of your index finger on the middle of the gun's trigger. It should be centered. If you're only placing the top edge of your finger or are over-grasping to the bend of the first knuckle, your shot will end up pulling to the left or right of your target.

With your finger properly placed, pull the trigger back in one smooth motion.

When you have the target in your sights and you're ready to fire, place your finger on the trigger. Your finger should not be on the trigger until you're fully ready to fire. The center of the first pad of your finger is what should touch the trigger.

If you only press with the tip of your finger, you'll push your shot inside. Holding the trigger inside the first knuckle joint will cause the handgun to push the shot to the outside.

With your finger placed correctly, press the trigger back in a straight and smooth motion. Use only the pad of your finger and bend the first two joints. Don't use any other muscles in your hand.

Learn about your gun's trigger reset.

Trigger reset is the distance the trigger moves back toward its "at rest" position before it resets, allowing the gun to be fired again. You don't need to let the trigger all the way out before squeezing it for your next shot.

Do not take your finger off of the trigger between shots. Moving your finger will change your placement, affecting your accuracy. Practice trigger reset by letting out the trigger slowly until you feel a break, or slight click. That is the trigger resetting. At this point you can squeeze the trigger for your next shot.

American Concealed

You can quickly overcome the obstacles to accuracy.

Flinching is one of the biggest obstacles to accuracy. It happens when, as you press the trigger, you anticipate the recoil and loud sound that associated with the shot.

When you anticipate the shot your hand will dip to counteract it. It is also common to close your eyes in anticipation of the shot. Blinking and squeezing your eyes will decrease your accuracy.

Clenching your hands as you squeeze the trigger grip is also a common reaction. Scattered shots all over or outside your target is a common result of clenching your grip.

Focus on breaking bad shooting habits.

Give your trigger a steady controlled press all the way back, focusing on your trigger squeeze and sight picture. Complete this as a dry-fire exercise. Let the sound and recoil of the shot surprise you.

When you've completed dry-fire exercises, it's time to move to the range. In your shooting stance, execute the same steady trigger squeeze we described earlier.

Practice frequently. The more you hear and feel the shot, you'll become more comfortable and will stop anticipating the shot.

Sight Alignment

The legendary lawman Wyatt Earp once said, "Fast is fine, but accuracy is everything." When you're under attack though, sometimes fast is all you get. Here's how to make the most of it.

The truth is, violent scenarios can take on any form. You might only have the time to fire fast and close, or you may need to line up a shot in a crowded area. If you want to be effective, you must learn to balance speed and accuracy to get the most effective shot.

In some cases, unsighted fire may be your only option.

In a violent attack, the threat is not often more than a few feet away. High accuracy isn't required in situations like these. A violent target at such close range only needs to be stopped as quickly as possible.

Point shooting is only as accurate as you can point a handgun as an extension of your arm. It's sometimes called "intuitive" shooting because in these situations you don't have the time to worry about accuracy, you just rely on your training and feel to get the best placement possible.

Flash Sight Picture

If your attacker isn't at close range you might have the chance to get a flash sight picture. You can increase your accuracy at this point since speed isn't as much of an issue.

When the threat has put your life in danger, your main focus will be on that. Bringing your sights in line with the target but focusing on the dangerous target instead is called getting a flash sight picture.

Front Sight Focus

In exchange for speed, you can increase your accuracy with sighted fire. It can be the most difficult of the three options, mostly because accuracy requires regulated breath, the ability to maintain proper grip, and your eyes to focus clearly on your gun's sights.

Your gun's front sight is clearly aligned to the target and is ready to deliver an effective shot across a much longer distance. That distance could be filled with any number of things in a chaotic scenario, so accuracy is vital.

Include different scenarios and sight pictures in your training. Remember that an attack won't be anything like target practice at the range, so be comfortable moving between speed and accuracy.

What is Knockdown Power?

When it comes down to it, concealed carry means having the ability to stop a violent threat to your life or someone else's life as soon as possible. Know the sides of the Knockdown Power argument before you wade in.

What is the role of velocity in Knockdown Power?

Kinetic energy is all about how much force the bullet has as its traveling. That's basically determined by looking at how fast it travels (feet per second, or FPS) and how much it weighs (bullet weight in grains). In this equation, velocity is the key.

That means that a 9mm, traveling around 1,400 FPS, would be a better bet than a .45 ACP, traveling around 1,100 FPS. One arrives at its target much faster but with less weight behind it.

One of the downsides to increased velocity is barrel length. As the barrel shortens FPS will go down as well.

Increase potential damage with Knockdown Power.

This side of the argument usually relies on the Taylor Knockout Factor (TKOF), which takes the equation above and adds in the diameter of the bullet.

Obviously, a larger bullet is going to do more damage to a target in the form of a bigger hole. Using this element of knockdown power, bigger calibers like a .40 S&W, weighing in at 180 grains, rank fairly high with a TKOF of 10.18. Compare that to the tiny .22, which packs a punch of TKOF 1.33.

In the end, accuracy equals effectiveness.

No matter what side of the knockdown power discussion you find yourself on, one well-placed shot will bring down an attacker faster than 10 off-target blasts. Your caliber could have the power to bring down a charging elephant, but if you can't find the target it won't do you a bit of good.

You should be carrying the most powerful caliber of handgun that fits you and your lifestyle. Larger caliber bullets can be expensive, and heavier handguns can be more difficult to carry everyday.

Take the time to research what you'll carry by reading up on the caliber and taking plenty of practice shots. It's up to you to decide what works best for you, because ultimately, any caliber used in self-defense is better than no caliber.

Part Four

Preventing and Surviving Self-Defense Scenarios

American Concealed

If you find yourself in a situation in which you feel your life or the lives of others is in immediate danger, you may need to use your concealed weapon to defend yourself. This is the one situation you never want to experience, but you must be prepared regardless.

It's important to know how to avoid such a situation in the first place. Situational awareness is an essential self-defense skill that is taught in many branches of the military and law enforcement. The best self-defense is to not be in places and situations where you'll find yourself threatened.

If the situation escalates or is unavoidable, be aware of the basic tactics for keeping yourself alive and unharmed. These threats often happen quickly and without warning. They require quick thinking and even quicker physical reactions. Practice and knowledge are the keys to performing these tactics effectively.

The legal aspects of self-defense are many. You're required to understand and work according to the laws of the state as well as use proper technique all during the high emotion and stress of a combat scenario. Knowing this, it's your job to be as prepared as possible before you leave the house with a concealed handgun.

Turn the Tables with Situational Awareness

The situations are all too familiar. While walking home from work you spot someone up ahead and you get a bad feeling. You're out with friends and a car slowly cruises past. The feelings we get when things might be dangerous are very real. Looking out for those moments and knowing what to do when they happen is called situational awareness, and it just might mean the difference between life and death.

Recognize the danger of distractions and other barriers to awareness.

Everyone is guilty of being a little too familiar with their surroundings sometimes. The places we sometimes think of as perfectly safe can still harbor dangers. It is in these places that we let our guard down and take a casual approach to our safety.

Another barrier to situational awareness is information overload. This really just means that you've got too many things going on at once. When you're distracted, things happen out of range of your radar and this could have bad results. If you're in a city or new place where lots of things are happening at once, choose a quiet store or cafe and get your bearings. Many people assume that a popular public event like a festival or sporting event are safe because there are lots of people around. Thieves actually target people in these situations because the high levels of noise, confusion, and distractions make an excellent cover.

Other barriers are the result of other influences. Fatigue, stress, or intoxication are often factors in self-defense situations. Those who choose to assault others look for people who are distressed and who may be unable to defend themselves. If you're intoxicated you lose a crucial ability to monitor your surroundings and reaction time drastically slow.

Stay aware in every environment.

There are a few quick actions to take to ensure that you are aware of your situation and your surroundings no matter where you are. This doesn't mean that you need to walk through your life being afraid of what's around every corner, it simply means that you make it a point to be aware of who is nearby and being confident of your actions.

You can apply these rules to times when you're alone as well as when you're with a group of people. Sometimes we can feel like we're safer when we're out with a few other people, but this doesn't mean you can stop paying attention to what's happening in your vicinity.

First, be clear on your objectives. This really means that you shouldn't leave without knowing where you're headed and how to get there. When you're out, walk with confidence and keep your head up.

American Concealed

Keeping your nose in your smartphone or blocking out all sound with pounding headphones can make you an attractive target.

If you're with a group of people, make sure that everyone knows where they're headed and you have each other's phone numbers in case you get separated.

After you are clear on where you're going and how you'll get there, the next objective is to continually be aware of your surroundings. This requires observant and assertive behavior. Keep your vision straight-ahead but be aware of movement, darkness, and other actions that are occurring in your peripheral vision.

When you're walking alone or with a group of people, stay focused on getting to where you're going. If your group can't decide where to go next or you think you might be lost, go into a nearby business and make a new plan, don't stand around looking into your phone or map. Finally, trust your gut! If you're picking up a bad vibe from a certain person or place, move yourself out of the area.

Your instincts when it comes to danger are actually pretty keen. If you're getting the feeling you shouldn't be somewhere, the best idea is to act on it. If you find out later that there was no danger, you can always head back and go exploring.

Concealed carry in doesn't make dangerous environments safer.

Don't have "Gun Courage." Anyone who carries a concealed handgun for protection should be mindful of its influence on their behavior. Being armed with a deadly weapon is no excuse for exploring areas and situations that are dangerous.

Take every opportunity to keep yourself safe by maintaining awareness of your surroundings. It's important to practice every aspect of concealed carry, and that includes paying attention to the people and places that could be a danger to you.

How to Stay Calm in Combat

When you holster your concealed handgun, your mind will likely run through a wide variety of possible situations and encounters. You can do your best to plan your day and take steps to avoid dangerous situations.

Regular training will keep your firing and reloading skills quick and sharp, but all of that could be rendered useless if you're not calm in the face of danger.

Popular television shows and movies show action heroes that calmly move through deadly situations, dodging bullets and dispatching bad guys with robotic efficiency. Hopefully, it comes as no surprise that real world combat is nothing like that. Looking a dangerous person in the face or fighting for your life is never a pretty scene.

It's a dirty scene filled with confusion, panic, and fear. No one survives physical threats and danger without sustaining some trauma, whether it's emotional or physical damage. You don't have to learn how to act like an action hero on a movie screen to know how to manage yourself in a combat situation. Preparing yourself and practicing is the best way to survive a situation that puts you in danger.

What's the worst thing you can do in a self-defense situation?

Nothing. If you haven't prepared yourself for how to handle combat, you can freeze up and find yourself unable to make a decision. Stress can hurt your ability to defend yourself. You can make poor choices and, even worse, have poor aim when it counts.

If you can't avoid being attacked, you'll need to take specific steps to protect yourself. These situations are the reason that you practice drawing, firing, and reloading your concealed handgun regularly.

Breathing is central to survival.

The foundation of surviving combat is to keep breathing. Stress makes your heart pound and your pulse race. If you're in danger, you may either stop breathing or hyperventilate. This obviously puts you at increased risk by shutting down your vital body responses.

Keep your breath steady and smooth. If you have the opportunity, force yourself to concentrate on only your breath. Taking even 30 seconds to bring your breathing into order can help to replenish oxygen and calm your mind. You'll supply your brain with the oxygen it needs to form plans and execute tasks.

You can learn to manage your breathing through practice. While at home or in minor stress situations at work or in the car, regulate your breathing by counting to three as you inhale and exhale. Be mindful of your breaths and how rapid or slow they are.

Practice slowing your breath down. If you have access to an outdoor firing range, you can do push ups or jumping jacks, or take a short run before you pick up your weapon and fire. This will help you experience how it will feel to be under stress.

Maintain a strong grip on your handgun from start to finish.

Several things can happen if you do not keep a strong grip on your handgun during combat. You increase the possibility of an attacker knocking it out of your hands, rendering you defenseless. Your grip must be strong and confident. Use your training and control to keep your finger off of the trigger unless you must destroy your target.

You can practice this at the range and at home. While firing your weapon at the range, accept the recoil and let it raise your grip and gun naturally. Return your hands to firing position and maintain your sight alignment on your target.

When you're at home, ensure that the gun is unloaded and safe to handle, then practice gripping and releasing the gun appropriately to train your mind and hand to recognize the features of the gun without the benefit of sight.

Use the best shooting stance that you can manage.

A critical defense situation is very different from target practice. You're just trying to use the gun as well as possible in a fight, not keep perfect body positioning. When you feel threatened, it's natural to lean slightly forward and put your weight on the balls of your feet. Maintain bent knees and straight arms. Remain athletic and this will make you more resistant to being knocked over. Bent arms can make the gun less reliable by raising the muzzle upon firing and disrupting the gun's ability to chamber the next round.

It's crucial that you practice drawing and firing your gun from a variety of positions and stances. Practice firing and reloading while also moving, as you may need to avoid return fire or manage attackers from different directions. If possible, practice firing from the ground as well.

Staying out of conflicts requires self-discipline.

Remember that many self-defense scenarios often start out as small and avoidable conflicts. One of your main responsibilities is to do all you can to avoid getting into dangerous situations. Don't let arguments escalate into fights. If the other person asks you to "take this outside" or taunts you into hitting them, don't take the bait. If you accept the invitation you'll have trouble proving that you acted in self-defense.

Of course, there are many incidents that happen without any warning and there's nothing you could do to stop the attack. You can take all the steps necessary to stay out of danger but sometimes it comes looking for you. Be smart about the people you socialize with and be sure to keep quality company.

When you make an expensive purchase, post personal news on social media, or let loose at a party, the people who are close to you can either protect you or take advantage of you. If you're not careful, you can set yourself up for an attack by allowing a malicious person to know details about your life.

American Concealed

When a threat is nearby though, managing your body's natural reactions to danger will help you to stay calm in combat. Your body is built to protect itself, so work with it to survive. Practicing steady breathing and relaxation exercises will keep your mind calm and clear. A strong and practiced grip and a dynamic shooting stance can keep you alive in the most dangerous of situations.

What Happens Inside Your Body During a Violent Attack?

What happens to your brain and body when you're facing a threat to your life? When you know what to expect, you won't be as debilitated when you go through the experience.

Your brain functions differently when fear sets in.

When you first feel frightened or surprised by a assumed threat, a signal shoots to your amygdala, which is the part of our brain that controls emotion, memory, and decision-making.

The signal moves so fast that it bypasses any chances to think with logic. This is the reason why a dangling Halloween decoration can manage to scare you out of your shoes when you really know that it's nothing to fear.

Your brain initiates its fight or flight response once a threat is perceived. Your body is flooded with adrenaline and cortisol, both determined to provide energy to endure the stressful situation.

Distorted vision can alter your perception.

Extreme fear and distress can cause significant changes to your vision. During a violent encounter, your brain is struggling to process a flood of information, so some senses can be heightened while others may not seem to be working at all.

When you're under attack, tunnel vision causes your brain to concentrate on specific details rather than taking in the entire scene. Victims of violent attack often report that their attacker was much closer or farther away than they actually were.

You can fight the memory loss after an attack.

The greater the amount of stress in the event, the more difficult it will be to accurately recall the details. The attack can overload your senses and cause memory loss associated with the incident.

A restful night's sleep and calm outlook can help to restore memories of a violent incident. If you're a witness or victim to an attack, accurate recall of the event is critical to bringing the attacker to justice and explaining any self-defense actions.

Consider the Many Options for Personal Protection

You should only fire a gun in self-defense if you feel that your life is in immediate danger. The reality is, in many violent scenarios your life is not being threatened. At least not initially. You should take steps to defend yourself in a non-lethal way if at all possible.

There are situations and threats to your safety that don't always require a firearm. Going for a jog or bike ride on a neighborhood path isn't exactly conducive to concealed carry.

Also consider the difference between someone who is being annoying or belligerent, but not necessarily acting in such a way that you fear for your life. You'll need non-lethal methods of ending the situation before it escalates.

Pepper Spray

For the price and availability, you won't find a better option for non-lethal self-defense than pepper spray. It's cheap and very effective in a variety of situations. Let's look at how to choose pepper spray and how to use it effectively.

Pepper spray is a non-lethal self-defense weapon used by military and police personnel but is also popular with regular civilians. It contains the same chemical that makes peppers spicy and hot, oleoresin capsaicin. This chemical is an extremely painful irritant and causes serious pain in humans as well as threatening animals like dogs or even bears.

When it makes contact with an attacker's face, it causes intense burning and irritation in the eyes and eyelids. It also causes difficulty breathing and swelling, making it difficult to see and function. Some sprays feature a red dye that stains the attacker's face and clothes, facilitating identification by law enforcement.

Different sprays offer a variety of features to consider. Most spray to a range between 8 and 20 feet. Pepper spray is no different from any other self-defense weapon in that it is typically used in circumstances in which an attacker is very close.

The contents of the spray are powerful enough to disable you as well, so look for a spray that is accurate enough to give you room to avoid the spray but also keep a threat at a distance.

Likewise, different sprays have a different capacity for the number of shots that can be used. The range varies widely from just a few shots to 30 or more. This mainly affects the size of the cannister you use, so consider where you'll be carrying and what type of situations you expect to find yourself. The larger capacities are used mostly for military or law enforcement scenarios in which multiple attackers would need to be subdued quickly.

Generally, a good suggestion is to choose a size and shot capacity that fits best with your lifestyle. Pepper spray is powerful enough to disable a very strong person for at least 15 or 20 minutes with a direct shot to the face, but if you're facing a group of three or four threats, you could conceivably use 10 to 15 shots to keep yourself safe. In the case of shot capacity, it's better to err on the side of caution and carry as large a container as is convenient for you.

When you use pepper spray, remember that it's only effective if it makes contact with an attacker's face. Spraying any other body part with pepper spray does nothing more than create a noxious cloud that puts you in just as much danger as the attacker. This is one of the disadvantages of pepper spray, and why it shouldn't be the only self-defense weapon you carry.

In order to be the most effective, fully extend your arm in the direction of the attacker's face. An ideal defensive spray would line the attacker's face from ear to ear, though even slight contact with the cheeks is enough to cause discomfort. Continue to spray until the threat is totally incapacitated, but do not move forward in the direction that you've sprayed.

After the threat is eliminated, move away from the area. It is common for the person who used the spray to still feel some of the effects, but only minimally if you're able to clear the area.

Just as with any weapon, you must test and practice using pepper spray in order to be accurate and fast. Never test the spray indoors or in close proximity to pets or children. Test your spray in an open, well-ventilated area with the breeze blowing away from you. Aim your spray at a target like a tree in order to practice making accurate contact with an attacker.

Read and follow the directions on the spray carefully. Even though pepper sprays are not lethal, they can cause severe pain and can clear out an entire house if used indoors.

Tactical Flashlights

You can make a concealed handgun into an even more effective self-defense tool by pairing it with a tactical flashlight. This isn't just your usual plastic flashlight, though. Tactical flashlights are built for military and law enforcement use.

American Concealed

They're tough enough to handle combat situations and all kinds of emergencies. Research has shown that most armed attacks occur in low light, so keeping a flashlight on you is a great self-defense tactic. A flashlight can be an effective deterrent to an attacker.

A flashlight takes away darkness, which an attacker might try to use for an advantage. Use your tactical flashlight before an attack occurs by keeping one on you for those times when you find yourself in a low light environment. If you use it to illuminate any dark areas around corners or under cars as you're walking you take away the element of surprise.

Don't keep your light on the entire time, as an attacker may aim the attack at the light. Using the light to briefly scan the area and then turning it off to move along not only keeps an attacker confused but also allows your eyes to stay adapted to the darkness.

After drawing your handgun, you want to be 100% sure of what you're firing at and why.

Don't pull the trigger if you're unsure of your target or your immediate surroundings.

Holding your flashlight below your gun can illuminate your target but not your gun sights. Use your non-dominant hand to hold the light beside your head or at your chest and extend your gun with your other hand, keeping both your target and sights in the light.

If you're unarmed and attacked while carrying a tactical flashlight, train the beam at the attacker's eyes. If it's bright enough it will be enough to temporarily blind them and disorient them.

Use a flashlight that has at least 120 lumens (you can easily find some with 500 or more) for maximum brightness. With the light trained on the attacker's eyes, use kicks to the legs and groin to defend yourself and disable the attacker. Tactical flashlights are rugged enough to be an improvised weapon.

Their sturdy construction can withstand being smacked against the head and fingers of anyone trying to do you harm. Use one that is lightweight and easy to grip in high-stress situations. Look for a light with a bezel option to add additional striking power.

Tactical flashlights are inexpensive and simple to use. They are useful for self-defense and for other emergencies like power outages. If you're carrying concealed, keeping a flashlight with you will improve your aim in low light conditions and discourage would-be threats.

Preventing a Home Invasion

You hear the smash of glass and the sound of someone entering your home. Your pulse quickens and your eyes scan your possessions and your loved ones who are also scared. What happens when everyone looks to you for help? You need a plan and a way to protect yourself.

Luckily, there are specific steps you can take in order to make your home more safe. After some planning and practice you and your loved ones will be ready for anything.

The very first step in protecting your home from a potential invasion is to sit down and make a plan for the whole family.

It's essential that you involve everyone living with you at the time, be it family or roommates. Everyone should have a say and should understand the importance of their assigned role in the plan.

Everyone should have a role and a job to do in the plan, even if it's just to go to a certain room and stay there. After everyone has their assignments, make sure to practice occasionally and even in the dark. If each person has one thing to remember, they'll act quickly and with purpose.

It can help to choose a short phrase or word that lets everyone know that it's time to execute the safety plan that you've created. When they hear the phrase, they should know exactly where to go and what to do. Using a phrase like, "It's an emergency" or something similar lets even your youngest know that it's time to move without any explanations.

The second step is one you should have already considered. Keep your defensive firearm accessible and secure.

This means that you have chosen one particular firearm that you'll keep nearby that's loaded with self-defense ammunition. Keep it secure from children by using a premium quick access gun safe. The location of this defensive firearm shouldn't change and you should be able to locate it quickly and in the dark. Practice moving through the house with your weapon so that you're familiar with the hallways and doors you'll encounter in the event of an intruder.

You should always consider your neighbors and friends when you make your home invasion plan.

This is an element that is often overlooked because it seems like these people would never want to hurt you in any way. Many home invasions and robberies are done by people who are close to the family. They usually know your schedule, when you're out of town on vacation, and maybe even where you keep your valuables.

Be careful about who you talk to about your trips or recent purchases. Neighbors and friends you thought you trusted could be motivated by any number of factors that make them choose your property.

Make sure that no one enters your home without first identifying themselves and after you've had a look at them. Some intruders will knock desperately at your door in the middle of the night as a tactic for gaining entry.

If you don't know them, let them know you've called the police and they're on their way to give them assistance. Never let an unidentified person into your house.

There are a few other options for home defense to consider. They might seem unusual, but every home situation is unique. Take the time to analyze your current living area to find an option that works best for you.

Armed Self-Defense Handbook

A barking dog alarm as a theft deterrent.

A barking dog alarm can be electronically triggered to create loud barking sounds and is a great way to send would-be intruders packing before they even enter. The sounds of any dog, no matter the size, means that neighbors can be awakened and there is potential for injury waiting on the other side of the door.

One room in your home designated as a safe room.

Keep a charged cell phone, a few supplies like water and snacks, and self-defense weapons in this room. Reinforce the solid door with a bolt lock so that you're protected from anyone determined to get to you.

A small video camera to capture any intrusion.

There are many different varieties of small cameras, "nanny cams" and other similar kinds. Most of them are reasonably priced and easy to use. They just might be the evidence you need to prove your need for self-defense or to catch an intruder that got away.

When an intruder is invading your home they could be motivated by desperation, drugs, or any number of other factors. They aren't thinking clearly and only care about what is directly in front of them.

Do your best to stay calm and follow the plan you have put in place. Some of the valuables in your home may be damaged or stolen, that is something to understand right away. Ultimately, your life and the lives of others are the most important thing and no intruder should ever be able to take them without a fight.

What Intruders Look For When Choosing a Home to Invade

An attacker won't always be out in the streets, waiting for you to pass by. They may bring the danger right to your doorstep by invading your home. Most thieves will wait until they think no one is home before they enter, wanting to get in and out without any trouble. The likelihood of someone entering your home regardless of if it's occupied or not grows as times grow more and more desperate.

Home is a place where you should feel comfortable and safe. Your family deserves to live in a place that is free from danger. Keeping a firearm for protection at home is an effective way to keep your possessions and your loved ones safe, so take the steps to be sure you're prepared for a home invasion.

The intruder who breaks into your home wants the crime to be easy and fast. Smart thieves take the time to look at different properties. They know that spending some time looking at different properties can result in a bigger score.

It's also very common that the unlawful intruders are people that you know. They have been inside your home and they know what's inside. They also know about any security measures you take (or don't take).

What factors do thieves look for when choosing a home to invade?
- Newspapers, fliers, and mail that hasn't been collected.

- Lights and televisions that are off for days at a time.

- Lawns and gardens that are overgrown.

- Knocks to the door that go unanswered.

- Staff like painters, gardeners, or pest control that visit the home on a schedule.

- Your social media profile to see when you're on vacation.

- No evidence of a dog.

- Evidence of large expensive purchases in the garbage.

Keeping these warning signs in mind, there are some small things you can do to make your home unattractive to intruders. The second they see that they might need to contend with an obstacle, they'll think twice before entering.

Keep hunting-themed stickers on your vehicles. This is a first signal to an intruder that odds are good that a firearm is waiting inside. A pair of large hunting or work boots beside the door can be a small suggestion that someone large is inside. Sometimes that's enough.

Even if you don't own a dog, some large dog toys in the yard or within view of windows and doors could be enough to discourage an intruder.

If someone knocks at the door, ask them to identify themselves. You're never obligated to open the door if the visitor makes you uncomfortable. If repeated visits are never answered, the intruder may assume nobody's home and enter.

Take the time to keep your property orderly and maintained. An unkempt yard and driveway could mean that there's no security or that no one has been home for an extended time.

Remember, you're not helpless against an attack. Start by looking for places around your property that could be an appealing spot for an attacker to hide. The property around your home has a lot to say to anyone willing to read the messages. Be aware of your surroundings when you enter and leave your home.

What to Do When You Know an Intruder is in Your Home

There may be absolutely nothing you can do to stop an intruder from entering your home. If they're desperate enough, an intruder may pose as a respectable service person and give a believable reason why they need to enter. They might be a family friend who visits and unlocks a window so that they can return later.

An intruder may be so desperate that they enter your home even if someone could be inside. They may have guessed wrong about your home being unoccupied. Either way, you may come face to face with the intruder.

- Avoid the intruder if at all possible. Don't yell out or go searching for them.

- Call 911, stay locked down, and be prepared to engage.

- Stand opposite of the door armed with the deadliest weapon you can find.

- If you fear for the lives of yourself or your family, aim to incapacitate and injure grievously.

- Know your target and surroundings before pulling the trigger.

If you can't hide or avoid contact with the intruder, protecting your life and the lives of others should be your first priority. Every critical scenario is different and it's impossible to predict what you or the intruder will do when it actually occurs. All you can really do is try your best to prepare yourself and your family for the situation.

Use your firearm only if you feel that your life is in danger and you have no other options. Follow your state's laws concerning Stand Your Ground, Castle Doctrine, or Duty to Retreat. We'll cover those in a later chapter.

Armed Self-Defense Handbook

Remember that intruders are often unwilling to fight or die for the valuables in your home. The mere sight of a firearm could be enough to scare them away.

If you're able to set off your car alarm from your keys it may draw enough attention to deter the intruder.

What to Do in an Armed Robbery

How many stores and businesses do you enter during the week? Because it's such a regular part of life, it could be tough to count or even remember. Here are some suggestions for how to react if you're ever caught in the middle of an armed robbery while in a store.

- *Take cover in a secure location.*

    Don't resist when a robbery occurs. Move to a place where you are protected but still have a view of the threat. The longer you delay a robbery, the more you increase the chance for violence.

- *Be sure of your target.*

    Armed robberies usually happen quickly with no warning. Thieves in plain clothes acting as inconspicuous as possible look very much like any other customer in the store. Be sure of how many threats there are and their location.

- *Know what's behind and near your target.*

    If you find yourself with the opportunity to fire and end the violent threat, do so only when innocent customers are not in danger and you can take a clear shot.

American Concealed

- *Fire only when your life, or the life of another person, is in immediate danger.*

   The cash or electronics in a store are none of your concern. You must be ready to observe the situation and quickly evaluate the threat. Keep in mind that you are not helpless. You can observe the person, what they touch, and their vehicle and that information and that can also help in the end.

- *Shoot to end the threat as quickly as possible.*

   If there is a violent threat, eliminate it as quickly as possible. Aiming for the head or trying to injure only increases the odds of shots hitting innocent people or an injury that allows the gunman to keep firing. Shoot until there is no threat present.

- *Respect and work with arriving law enforcement.*

   Stay in the store until law enforcement arrives. Place your gun on the floor, cooperate, and be respectful. These officers only want to be sure that everyone is safe, and they have no knowledge about you or the incident other than being called to respond.

   If you've chosen to carry a firearm for protection, it's best to first talk with an attorney about how to handle these potential circumstances, then work with a certified firearms instructor to learn how to use your handgun effectively.

How to Survive an Active Shooter

   In an active shooter situation, an individual is using a weapon to harm or kill people in a public space. You need to know what to do if there is an active shooter near you. An active shooter is unpredictable and very dangerous. These situations are chaotic and scary. Things can quickly escalate to a deadly level. Below are three ways to survive an active shooter event.

If possible, get out and stay out.

Escape the area as quickly as possible when there is an active shooter, but do not put yourself in the path or sight of the individual. If you have bags and other belongings, leave them behind. Other people may not want to leave with you. Leave them behind as well.

In an active shooter event, you must commit to your decisions and trust that you will be more likely to survive. Once you have left the situation, do not go back inside to rescue others. Contact law enforcement and let trained professionals handle the situation.

Find a place to hide low and stay under cover.

Stay low and find a place to hide if escaping would put you in sight of the active shooter. Close the doors and blinds if you are in an office or school building. Get behind large objects to provide cover and protection. Lock any doors that the active shooter might use.

Be quiet and do not do anything to provoke the active shooter. They are unpredictable and you should not try to negotiate with them. An active shooter is not using logic or reason.

Take the shooter down with supreme aggression.

Escaping or hiding may not be an option for you if there is an active shooter in a public space. You should only use aggression on the active shooter if you have no other choice for survival. When you do so, act with swift aggression.

Harm the shooter as severely as you can and without any reservations. Throw or use any object you can find as an improvised weapon. If another person will help you, make a plan for how to take the active shooter down as quickly as possible and then commit to it.

Busy public spaces and office buildings are targets for an active shooter who wants to harm as many people as possible in a short amount of time. Know exactly what you will do when you are in a potentially dangerous situation.

What to Do if You're Attacked in or Near Your Car

Think about all of the ways you are vulnerable to an attack in your car. Preparing for the worst scenarios will keep you and your family safe when there is a threat. Are you ever in these situations?

Drivers and passengers are frequently getting in and out of vehicles, and vulnerability is highest at these times.

Vehicles are used for commuting to work or for running errands, and this means that drivers are almost guaranteed to have a wallet, purse, or other valuables that have been purchased easily accessible in the vehicle.

You own an expensive car or truck that others might want. Consider also the value of the vehicle itself, and that a highly motivated attacker may want to take it from you.

Some simple parking strategies can increase safety

No matter where you're going to or coming from, you'll need to park your car. Being alert as to how and where you park your car is the best way to stay prepared.

When arriving at home, park as close to home as possible. If you're pulling into your garage, maintain awareness of your garage door and anyone who may enter it as you enter. Garages are wonderful, but anyone wanting access can get you, your vehicle, and your home all in one entrance. Be aware of the opportunities for attackers that your garage presents.

Avoid parking in locations far from your destination or in areas with poor lighting. Being in a hurry and taking the first spot you see can be a bad choice. It is always worth the extra time searching when you consider the potential threats.

If you are driving family and friends to a destination, you will probably be carrying protection if you carry on a regular basis. As the driver, you can drop your loved ones off at the door and then proceed to find a place to park. This keeps them safe and allows you, the driver carrying concealed, to handle a threat should one present itself.

There are some things you can do to stay protected while driving.

You are most safe from threats while in a locked car that is moving, but that doesn't mean that you are out of danger entirely. Traffic during rush hour or holidays presents a few threats. There are many more drivers on the road, many of them feeling tired or stressed. This means that potential attackers have more vehicles from which to choose.

It can also increase your risk of attack in a "road rage" situation. It always pays to have a full gas tank. Be sure to stay fueled up for a few reasons. First, you want to be able to drive away from any potential threats, as the best way to handle these situations is simply to avoid them if at all possible.

Second, you don't want an empty tank to determine where you fill up. A poorly lit and empty gas station can present many threats, so keep to the places you know and trust.

Drawing and firing from the driver's seat can protect you and your passengers.

Start your preparations by informing yourself of the local and state laws about firearms inside your vehicle. Learn about where and how exactly you can store your handguns while driving. Regulations differ from state to state, but store your handgun in the most accessible location while driving.

American Concealed

Practice locating and drawing your weapon. Consider the location of your seat belt, steering wheel, and middle console. Practice your movements until they feel fluid and fast. Now this type of defense has some particular movements and types of fire that are very unique. You may need to fire through your car windows.

The confined space makes it incredibly loud. Vehicle windows will shatter if you need to fire through them, just be aware that windshields are built to survive contact much more than passenger windows. Attackers in rear seats are vulnerable to shots fired through seats.

A seatbelt and a well-constructed front seat means more safety in the event of a vehicle crash, but unfortunately also means that you don't have much room for movement in the event you need self-defense.

We spend lots of time in our vehicles. Mostly we are just driving around town or to and from work. Don't take the regularity of your drive for granted. Prepare for any situation or threat that may occur in or around your vehicle. You make sure that your car is safe in the event of a crash, but make sure you are protected from other threats as well.

How to Carry Concealed in Bars and Restaurants

Residents of some states can now be armed for self-defense in establishments that serve alcohol, provided there's a restaurant on-site. These changes usually come amidst a steady increase in concealed carry permits in the state.

If you're carrying in places where alcohol is served, keep some very important things in mind. You could save yourself some serious trouble by knowing the law, and your limits.

Know your state's laws concerning possession of firearms where alcohol is sold.

Some states' laws on this issue differ based on where and how much food is sold. Every state has specific rules for all things concerning alcohol. Don't assume that laws are consistent from county to county. Most employees and patrons are probably unaware of the laws that apply in the establishment.

Expect patrons who see printing or a visible handgun to be wary of you and suspect the worst. Remain respectful of employees who have not been informed of the law.

If the law says keep it concealed, keep it concealed. Acting irresponsibly or carrying incorrectly might lead to an incident that makes lawmakers, and the public they represent, reconsider.

Know your limits.

There is nothing wrong with being armed for self-defense while enjoying time with family and friends, but being responsible is of the utmost importance.

Remove yourself from the area if you think you're unable to be precisely accurate and make sound choices. Every alcoholic drink you consume diminishes your ability to be effective.

Know the legal implications of carrying firearms in bar.

If anyone wants to take the fight outside, don't take up the offer. The second you willingly engage in violence, you will have serious trouble proving that you needed to defend yourself.

If you're intoxicated and choose to fire a handgun anyway, you could be knowingly putting innocent lives in danger. You've willingly put yourself in a place that serves alcohol, so it's up to you to make good choices.

Simply put, alcohol and guns don't mix. Every time you holster your concealed firearm, you must hold yourself to a higher standard of responsibility.

Part Five

The Legal Aspects of Self-Defense

American Concealed

An essential element of responsible concealed carry is the knowledge of the legal aspects of self-defense. Arming yourself with the appropriate weapon is not enough. Target practice at the range is not enough. You must take the time to research and learn what your state of residence says about concealed carry. Every state is different, so what one person says doesn't always apply to your situation. In this book, we can outline some of the major concepts, but it's up to you to do the research on your end.

It's not the glamorous or fun side of gun ownership, but it can save you plenty of time, money, and confusion if you ever find yourself in court or other legal dispute. Reading up on local laws and federal restrictions takes time and isn't nearly as fun as popping off rounds at the range, that's for sure. But it's essential that all of us do our due diligence and devote time to reading up on current news and discussions of gun law around our country.

You might find that you disagree with how the gun laws are set up in your state. Remember that you also have an obligation to be an involved citizen. If you feel that the current laws are prohibitive of your rights as a gun owner, contact your government representatives by email, phone, or make an appointment to meet with them at their local offices.

As an informed and respectful citizen, you have more power to change the laws than you think. Be resourceful and put together a group of gun owners who share your thoughts. It's not only your right to make your voice heard in your government's decisions, it's your responsibility.

What to Do After an Armed Self-Defense Incident

There is plenty to read and practice when it comes to protecting yourself when attacked. You can attend classes, watch videos, and read up on proven strategies. All of those strategies are definitely a good way to be prepared, but they leave out some crucial information.

Armed Self-Defense Handbook

What you do immediately after successfully defending against an attacker can end up being even more important than how you survived in the first place. It is sad to see it this way, but for many attack survivors, the battle continues long after the threat is gone.

If you don't handle the situation properly from the beginning, you could face a long legal process that can cause personal and financial problems for years to come.

The terror of a deadly assault has passed, but that doesn't mean the situation is finished. There are steps you must take after you've ended a potential threat with deadly force or convincing the threat to leave the scene.

You've ended the threat by either displaying your concealed firearm or causing serious injury to your attacker.

At this point, your first step is to determine that a threat is no longer present. Survey the area to see if any threat still exists and escape if necessary. If there is no longer a threat, look over yourself and assess yourself for any injury you may have sustained. The high stress and adrenaline levels during the attack may have hidden the pain of injury.

Call 9-1-1 as soon as safely possible. If someone has sustained serious injury it is your responsibility to call and seek help. State your name and report that an attack has occurred. Clearly give the address and give the operator a description of the scene. Describe yourself as well as anyone who is injured.

Notify the operator that you are in possession of a firearm and have a permit to carry concealed. Inform them of the location of the firearm. If there is still a threat present, secure the firearm but have it ready to use again if needed. If the threat is incapacitated, place the weapon in full view of any approaching officer.

Politely end the call and contact your attorney. Most likely, you'll be told to resist any impulse you have to give a statement or explain the situation to the police. You've just been through a traumatic incident, you won't be thinking clearly and could end up saying something you don't mean or that can be taken the wrong way. Be respectful of the officers the entire time, and wait to talk until you have an attorney present.

Time is of the utmost importance at this point. You'll want to be the first to call and report the incident. Your attacker may attempt to call first and make you into the bad person in the situation by giving a biased report of the incident. It isn't right, but there is sometimes a bias that leans in favor of the first person to call. There is a feeling that a good person calls right away and a bad person avoids calling. Don't let this bias make you appear to be at fault.

Call your family and let them know what happened. Instruct them to stay silent on the matter until you've spoken with an attorney. If they call other friends and relatives or take to social media to express their feelings, these can all come back to hurt your case if you find yourself in a trial.

You've made the necessary phone calls and the dynamic threat of injury of death is no longer imminent.

Keep in mind that even though you know you are the good person, law enforcement arrives on the scene with no prior knowledge of the situation. Keep your hands fully visible and comply with all of their commands. This is not the time to argue or explain.

If you have the presence of mind to answer questions, give your best recollection of the attack. Point out any evidence that law enforcement may need to see. Identify any witnesses who may have seen what happened.

If you make the choice to remain silent, you must tell the officers that you are using your right to remain silent. Simply staying silent doesn't help anyone, and your refusal isn't respectful of the officer trying to handle the situation. You have the right to wait until an attorney is present and give a statement at that time.

If your mind is blank and you can't think of what do or say (which is a possibility given what you've just endured) simply be respectful and do not give any statements until an attorney is present.

Legal issues to consider in the aftermath of a self-defense incident.

It's easy to look into the future and assume that after defending yourself you'll be celebrated as a hero and brave model citizen. The sad fact is that it isn't unheard of to read about honest armed citizens who have found themselves in court.

In the worst case scenario you may find yourself spending thousands of dollars defending your actions or learning that your attacker is actually bringing legal action against you. Refer to your insurance policies to see what types of incidents involving a firearm are covered. You may also want to investigate Self-Defense Insurance as a strategy to alleviate the significant financial burden of court cases.

The Judicious Use of Deadly Force

Regular practice and an interest in guns is simply not enough. It's assumed that when you carry concealed you're also fully aware of the legal aspects of concealed carry and self-defense. The simple act of holstering a weapon for defense skyrockets your levels of responsibility.

None of what follows is intended to be legal advice. It's simply a broad overview to introduce you to some important legal aspects of concealed carry. We can offer insight into the legal basics, but it's up to you to learn the specific laws for your state of residence and your individual situation.

Deadly force is the last resort when your life's in danger.

Deadly force is a high level of force that a person can use in order to kill or cause serious bodily injury to an attacker when there is no other option. Below are three important aspects to deadly force that every gun owner should know.

Avoid dangerous confrontations if you can.

It's your responsibility to use good judgment and stay out of places and situations where your life might be in danger. Carrying a concealed handgun for protection is no reason to go walking into situations that you'd otherwise avoid. If a confrontation is brewing, do not provoke it. Take any opportunity to leave and keep your life and the lives of others intact.

How you define a threat makes all the difference.

An attacker can be a threat to your life in a few different ways. Overall, they have the ability to kill or harm you seriously. They could have a deadly weapon that they intend to use. They also may have other factors in their favor that put you in danger. They may outnumber you, be much more strong and physically able than you, or they might possess some other strength or skill like advanced martial arts. These advantages put you in danger.

The best defense is to "know before you go."

Every situation is different, and self-defense requires some quick mental gymnastics. If you possess the ability to defend yourself in a non-lethal manner, like martial arts training or pepper spray, you may have to justify why you didn't use it first. If you used deadly force on an attacker who was of equal or lesser physical ability than you, you may have explaining to do.

If you want to educate yourself even more about the legal aspects of concealed carry (and you should), talk with an attorney who can make the laws clear to you.

Armed Self-Defense Handbook

Carrying a concealed handgun gives us the power to defend ourselves and others if there is a threat to our lives. It's up to us to have a clear understanding of how the law influences our actions before we even holster our handguns.

The Castle Doctrine, Duty to Retreat, and Stand Your Ground

The legal issues concerning armed self-defense can be more complicated than you would assume. It is never cut-and-dry, and every situation has it's own elements that make it unique.

The common phrase, "I'd rather be judged by 12 than carried by 6" is popular on message boards and social media comment threads. It's sure sounds nice and simple but the fact is that the act of defending yourself with a gun carries with it some very serious legal concerns.

Anyone who just says that line is likely to be the same type to ignore the laws and requirements concerning the use of lethal force in their state. This is a serious mistake, as legal fees and time spent in court are extremely costly in both the bank account and the emotional toll on yourself and family. It's never as simple as a nice-sounding phrase.

No, it's not quite as fun as popping off rounds at the range, but familiarizing yourself with the laws surrounding concealed carry is just as vital as tactical practice. It can pay off in a serious way if you ever find yourself in the aftermath of a violent incident. Remember, every time you pick up your firearm you are expected to be aware of the many laws and restrictions that apply to you.

Below we'll offer a quick overview to introduce you to some basic legal concepts concerning armed self-defense. These will help you get started, but it's up to you to continue the search for more information that applies directly to you.

American Concealed

Castle Doctrine

This refers to an old English Common Law principle that considers a person's home to be his or her castle. According to Castle Doctrine (also sometimes called "Defense of Habitation"), a person had the right to defend their home if attacked there.

Some states have since accepted modern-day adaptations to this idea that have expanded the "castle" to include a person's car, yard, and even the workplace. Castle Doctrine has different interpretations from state to state, but most share the same basic principles. It should be common knowledge among property owners, regardless of gun ownership.

Hopefully, you'll never need to use Castle Doctrine as a defense while in court. It's a situation no one wants to experience. Enduring and surviving violence is never easy, but continuing to deal with the event through lengthy court battles is something you don't want to experience if at all possible.

Castle Doctrine is used a defense in court to justify the use of deadly force when attacked at home or other owned property.

Castle Doctrine is used when the attacker had no right to be in the home, and entered without permission of the owner.

In some states, this can also refer to a person's vehicle or workplace.

Duty to Retreat

In some states, citizens have what's called a "Duty to Retreat." This means that, when attacked, a person must try to retreat and escape the attack before defending themselves. This is of course if a safe retreat is even possible.

If a person feels threatened, they must leave the situation if at all possible and use deadly force only as a last resort.

Armed Self-Defense Handbook

Stand Your Ground

Many states have done away with this requirement to retreat, allowing citizens to defend themselves with deadly force if they had the right to be there and were acting within the law.

If the attacker stops the assault and attempts to flee, the defense will not cover shots fired at a retreating person.

When the attacker also has the right to be in the location of the incident, it must be determined which person was the aggressor.

This defense can be used regardless of where the attack took place, whether at home, in public, or at work, etc.

Anyone who owns property or carries a gun for self-defense should be familiar with these laws in respect to their state. What one state considers to be self-defense, another could consider to be murder or assault.

The wording of these self-defense laws changes frequently and states review laws regularly. In order to have the most current information, review the laws for your state of residence and speak with a licensed, experienced attorney.

Part Six

Skill Building and Practice

American Concealed

Carrying concealed requires an ongoing education. Laws and local regulations change just as frequently as elected leaders, and current events can shape public opinion overnight. Reading up on news and government debate is only half the battle, though. Physical readiness is what finally completes the circle of responsible concealed carry.

Take a quick minute to imagine yourself in the heat of a self-defense scenario. How does it play out for you? You easily take down the bad guy with quick ace shooting and everyone celebrates you as the hero?

Chances are, a deadly attack will not even be anything close to that. Sadly, television and movies have given us a skewed version of what these attacks are really like. In real life, an attack doesn't have the dramatic conversations, whirling martial arts, and timely conclusions. They're often quick, violent, and emotionally scarring events.

Attackers will do whatever it takes to gain the advantage on you, even if that means outnumbering you or even being someone who you know and trust.

The swiftness and stress of a deadly attack are real reasons why it's important to be physically prepared for an armed self-defense situation. Your body and mind go through periods of intense stress, and that can have a big impact on your muscles. Your muscles are what control your ability to defend yourself and fire accurately, so if they are out of shape you odds of survival drop.

What does it mean to be physically ready? It means that your brain and body are prepared for the demands of concealed carry and for combat. Your experiences and your upbringing may give you the confidence to carry every day, but your skills and your movements will grow rusty without regular practice and instruction.

It's important to remember that physical readiness is one of the skills most often overlooked by people who carry concealed. It's fairly easy to read about gun laws or talk with other gun owners about current events. It's much more difficult to visit the range regularly and to keep your mind and body in good physical condition.

You need to exercise regularly and maintain a healthy lifestyle in order to successfully defend yourself. Handguns are powerful weapons that require a strong grip and good posture to fire accurately, and attacks demand a level of physical strength you may not know you ever had. Put yourself in the best position for success by being physically prepared.

Build Muscle Memory for Increased Accuracy and Effectiveness

When seconds count, muscle memory can end up saving your life. It's sometimes confused with sports or workout techniques. It's actually more related to our thoughts and memories, and the power we build lies within the mind, not the muscles.

When you execute a task repeatedly, you're reinforcing the memory of how to complete that task. When the time comes to complete the task you're able to do it quickly and efficiently, eliminating the need for conscious thought.

You've built up considerable muscle memory already, easily driving through intersections, typing in passwords, and getting dressed. Carrying concealed is no different. These actions require constant practice so that the movements are fast and familiar.

Most critical self-defense incidents will probably take place in very close proximity and will happen quickly. In times of high stress, we act almost without thinking. The brain tells the body to survive and doesn't spend extra time weighing the higher philosophy of the incident. We've all heard the phrase "practice makes perfect," but what if that's actually the cause of firing mistakes and unsafe practices? What if what you've learned all along is actually false?

The truth is, practice doesn't always mean perfection. If your practice involves poor technique, you're just teaching your mind bad habits. The sad part? The more you repeat bad firearm handling habits, the more difficult it will be to correct them.

Your muscles and mind do not know proper technique. It's your job to teach them the correct movements from the start.

The best way to build or correct your firearm handling is to break each process down into small segments. Learn the correct technique for each segment of the process and master it.

Finally, combine the segments together and repeat the procedure over and over again until you're confident that you can execute it with very little effort and thought.

So, after you've practiced and mastered the fundamentals of defensive firing you can move on to more sophisticated tactical techniques, right? Not so fast. Even as you add to your bank of defensive techniques you must always spend time on the basics that make up the foundation of more advanced skills.

Make the Most of Your Practice at the Firing Range

The best handguns and the best holsters can't help you in a crisis situation if you haven't put in the practice to make them effective. Sure, it takes time and extra effort to head to the firing range frequently to stay in firing shape, but the payoffs can be immense in a combat scenario. It requires some extra money spent on targets and ammunition and maybe a firing range membership, but the confidence you'll bring to a conflict is priceless.

When you get to the range, don't just spend your time fiddling with new gadgets you bought or chatting with shooting buddies, get down to business and maximize your time. Spend time getting familiar with your various handguns.

Get comfortable with how they feel to hold and fire. Contrary to what some may think, it isn't all about the gun, either. How you position your body and how you handle movement while firing are essential elements to self-defense with a firearm.

Practice the essential skills repeatedly.

Start slowly, making sure that each movement that is required is efficient, then pick up speed. Your body and brain learn skills through a process that psychologists call "scaffolding." Each piece of the skill that you master helps to build and support the next. If you make sure that each movement you learn is based on a solid foundation of correct position and speed, you'll soon have a full exercise done swiftly and with precision.

Your mindset is crucial to your success. It never hurts to imagine yourself in a combat situation. Train with the ultimate goal in mind: defending yourself quickly and accurately when under stress. As much as possible, keep your eyes, mind, and body in tune with your training by staying focused on a goal for up to 15 minutes at a time.

After that time is up, step back and take a quick break. Relax your mind and body. Have a quick drink of water and a light snack to keep your energy up. Then start another round of practice.

Practice various movements.

The movements required to move from a resting position to a ready position and then to a firing position are essential to practice. Attackers aren't going to present themselves politely at times when you are positioned in a firing stance.

The conditions could be very hasty, confusing, and panicked. The light may be low, you may be carrying a briefcase, or have children alongside you. Take these possible scenarios into account when you practice at the range.

Considering the close range in which you'll probably engage an attacker, maintain a distance of around seven to 10 feet from your target.

American Concealed

Practice transitioning from a relaxed position to locating your firearm and eventually sighting it on the target. Repeat this as many times as necessary to get comfortable. Adjust your holster and ammunition as much as needed for maximum efficiency.

Consider setting up multiple targets.

Frequently, attackers are not alone and may have a plan for overtaking their target. Keep in mind that unloading your entire magazine on one target can have deadly consequences. Practice using your shots most effectively and maximizing the number of hits per target.

This is where relying only on an indoor range can end up having unintended consequences. They're perfect for certain training, but it's essential that you find an outdoor range that allows multiple targets and movement. This is a great way to simulate what armed self-defense requires in the real world.

Learn to fire while on the move.

A self-defense scenario is never slow and stationary. No attacker will wait for you to move first, nor will they allow you time to get comfortable. The act of firing while moving will take time to master, but it is worth the effort. Move from side to side with your pistol trained on the target.

Undeniably, you'll be trying to remove yourself from the dangerous situation, so practice firing while backing away from your target. You may sound strange to the others at the range, but don't be afraid to practice yelling or verbally notifying the imagined attacker that you have a gun and intend to use it. Crisis situations are seldom peaceful and quiet affairs.

Your practice time at the range pays off in many ways. Consider the outcomes if you are caught in a self-defense scenario and are unable to find your backup ammunition or fumble with your pistol at a crucial moment. Regular practice is essential to staying safe when armed with a handgun.

Preparing for Firing Range Practice

It's one of the central elements of concealed carry. Regular practice is what keeps skills sharp and the mind focused. It's what teaches your mind and body to work together, executing a flawless draw and trigger squeeze when it counts the most.

But, if you don't follow the rules of perfect practice, your range time will be wasted. Range time can be composed of many things, but the majority of it should be spent on activities to improve your overall effectiveness. The price of ammunition and the range fees aside, you don't want to spend your valuable time on the wrong elements of defensive firing.

Dress for any possible situation.

Clothes that keep you comfortable are essential for the firing range, but remember that they aren't usually what you're wearing when carrying. Shooters frequently wear what they feel most comfortable shooting in, and that could cause problems down the road. Plan ahead to wear clothes that fit well, especially around the arms and chest, and that don't restrict your movement.

Practice drawing and firing while wearing the uniform or the outfits you would normally wear. This helps you stay familiar with your draw and the gun's concealed location. When the moment arrives, you'll want to know exactly how your clothing feels and what it takes to access your weapon.

Indoor firing ranges can lead some shooters into a false sense of security. The temperature is controlled and the lighting is perfect. Do what you can to practice firing while wearing the clothes you'll be wearing in the current season.

If you're dealing with winter wind and snow, it's important that you practice drawing and firing while wearing a coat and extra layers of clothing. It's essential that you know how your clothing restricts or otherwise changes your movements to protect yourself.

Add variety to build skills.

No practice session is complete without a variety of skill-building drills. Don't be a victim of routine at the range. One of the best ways to build your skills is to vary exercises. It teaches your body and your brain to work together no matter what the situation.

Many people at the range shoot from a position of low ready, meaning that they've already assumed a solid grip on the firearm and have the target visually aligned. They calmly raise the gun and sight in. Shooting for accuracy in cases like these is is fine, but shouldn't be the primary exercise at the range.

Armed self-defense requires mental agility and emotional stability. Stay focused while you're at the range and set goals for your speed and accuracy.

Build muscle memory by going back to the basics.

Muscle memory is real, and building it pays off. As you move through familiar motions your brain learns to act without thinking. This is central to armed self-defense. When a crisis strikes, you don't want to waste valuable time and energy concentrating on finding your holster, clicking off the safety, and the rest of your total draw. When you build the total skill together and teach your mind and body through repetition, you'll be repaid with smooth and clean movements.

This process is best completed when the fundamental movements and decisions are perfected and safe. No matter how long you've been shooting, get back to the basics and refine your handling procedures. This is sometimes where novice shooters get stuck.

If you practice an incorrect movement repeatedly, it will be tough to go back and correct it. Be sure you're pulling off the technique perfectly right from the start, or go back and begin again.

Competition helps you to stay sharp and positive.

This final rule is often overlooked. One of the fundamental rules of handgun safety is to have a positive attitude when handling guns. If you're out shooting to blow off steam from a bad day or because you're feeling angry at someone, you should find a healthier activity.

Spending time at the shooting range should be a time where you prepare for a situation that you hope to never endure. Keep your mindset positive and be open to learning new skills. Nothing keeps things positive better than a little healthy competition.

Challenge your friends with an electronic shot timer or phone app that records firing speed. Become familiar with other types of firearms by trying out a friend's gun or renting a new piece at the range. Bring a small tape measure and compete for the closest group at different distances.

Follow these four rules of the range and you'll see your speed and accuracy increase. You'll also enjoy range time more, and that leads to more confident carry.

Analyzing Your Draw Sequence

Think about how often baseball players analyze their batting swing. It's an endless process of tweaking small movements to achieve a better result. Your draw sequence is the same—it takes time and repetition. It does take time, but perfecting your concealed carry draw sequence can pay off big dividends.

American Concealed

There are four parts to your draw sequence.

Your concealed draw sequence can be broken down into four distinct sections. Each of those sections contain quite a few individual movements, so it's best to analyze the movements themselves each as they occur. Follow these steps to break down your draw sequence.

1) *Taking your environment and your clothing into account is your first step. Be prepared for anything.*

Think about where your firearm will be located and ask yourself a few questions. Will you need to bend down to access an ankle holster or open a briefcase? Will you be wearing a coat in cold weather? Are items like a belt buckle or cell phone in the same path as your draw sequence?

Practicing at the range from an open, easily accessible holster won't do you much good if you'll be needing to un-tuck a shirt or open a purse in a moment of crisis. Add in a coat or a bag to make your draw to complicate things. How do you handle these new additions?

2) *Now you have located your concealed handgun and initiated a steady grip for the second step of your draw.*

Depending on the location of your weapon, you'll want to either draw up or out with the muzzle facing down and your finger along the frame, not on the trigger.

What is the position of your non-shooting hand? It should be located in the center of your body with the palm ready to accept the grip of the gun as you bring it up with your shooting hand. It's also ready to provide any additional self-defense that might be necessary during the attack.

3) *The weapon is presented and your stance is facing the attacker, as best you can of course. You move into the third step and bring your firearm into the best defensive position you can manage.*

What is the position of your knees and elbows? Try to maintain a relaxed but strong position with slightly bent knees and elbows. You should not be rigid but should be able to move as the attack requires. Your finger at this point is still not on the trigger unless you truly intend to fire.

4) *Your arms are fully extended and you have the sights trained on the immediate threat.*

Maintain smooth and slow breathing as best as you can given the situation. Regulated breathing not only helps your accuracy but will help to keep you as calm as possible.

You can't realistically maintain this fully extended firing position for more than about 10 seconds. Your adrenaline will be pumping for sure, but maintaining a confident grip and muscle strength is essential. As you can see, there is much more to a four-step draw sequence than you may think.

Carrying concealed presents additional elements to consider. No threatening scenario will be the same and you could be required to fire from either standing, seated, or ground positions. You don't wear the same clothing each day and may dress differently depending on the weather. Break down the steps of your concealed carry draw sequence in order to best practice them and address any problems.

Cartridge Malfunctions and How to Handle Them Safely

Your concealed carry firearm is what protects you from a threat that could end your life. You keep it cleaned and well-maintained because, when every second counts, you don't want it to fail you. In addition to your range training and regular practice, you should be familiar with one of the truths of shooting: cartridges will malfunction.

If a cartridge malfunction occurs while you're at the firing range, deal with it calmly and safely. These incidents have potential for injury, so it's crucial that you can recognize it and deal with it correctly. There are three types of cartridge malfunctions to be aware of.

A misfire can also be called a dud or a failure to fire.

When one occurs, you hear a clicking sound upon trigger pull. Keep the gun pointed downrange for at least 10 seconds. The reaction may be delayed and the bullet will end up firing after a few seconds. Stay in your firing stance for 30 seconds and if the cartridge hasn't fired, remove it and place it in water for disposal later at an appropriate location.

When you're looking into the cause of a misfire, you can go in two directions. The cause can be your ammunition or the gun itself. Low quality ammunition has a bad reputation for misfires, as do handloaded cartridges.

Before purchasing ammunition, read the reviews and ensure you're getting quality for your money. If your handloads are causing you misfire problems, you may need to improve the seating of your primers. Ammunition usually meets fairly high quality standards, so unless ammunition is old or has been degraded somehow, the issue lies within your firearm.

When the trigger is pulled, there is no reaction within the powder or primer of the ammunition. The firing pin could misaligned, failing to strike the primer upon trigger pull and never starting the ignition process. Firing pins can also be damaged or worn over time, so if your casings are not being struck adequately examine your firing pin for issues. **Hangfires** occur when you hear a clicking sound upon trigger fire, but after a short amount of time the gun fires.

A ***Squib Load*** means that a cartridge did not fire properly due to incorrect or poor quality powder. These can be identified by either lack of muzzle flash, lack of recoil, or lack of sound. Wait 30 seconds. Do not fire another round. Unload remaining rounds and inspect for defects.

Conclusion

American Concealed

Books like this are crucial additions to the public's general knowledge about firearms and how they can be used for self-defense. Another very important part of increasing the people's knowledge is the skill and composure of the gun owners themselves. Those carrying concealed and using firearms for recreation must follow strict rules of safety and respect at all times. This helps public perception of firearms and promotes their use as self-defense tools.

You have the right to take steps to defend yourself. Handguns are a highly effective option, but should only be used in the case of a serious threat to your life or the lives of others. Understanding the appropriate situations when using a gun to defend yourself is legal, and when it's illegal, is a central part of responsible gun ownership.

Much of what you've read in this book has been a review of tactics, gear, and things to consider for armed self-defense. It's been a primer, and maybe a refresher, for those considering using a gun to defend themselves. The next steps you take are crucial.

The most important thing you can do is to test and try the equipment and tactics you've read in this book. Put in the time to research your choices and work on shooting skills at the firing range...before carrying concealed.

Don't carry a concealed firearm for self-defense until you've reviewed all of your options for holsters and ammunition. Don't carry concealed until you're familiar with the legal aspects of carrying in your state and city. Don't carry concealed until you're familiar with the parts of your handgun and how to care for them. Don't carry concealed until you've practiced firing, reloading, and defending yourself at a safe firing range with an instructor.

Thank you for reading The Armed Self-Defense Handbook by American Concealed. You've just taken a huge step to making your community, and world, a safer place.

American Concealed

More Work by American Concealed

Handgun Safety Training: A Practical Guide for Operating Pistols and Revolvers

A full course offering handgun safety basics for every level in an easy eBook format. Enjoy and learn with over 40 pages packed with foundational firearm ownership basics, proven concealed carry tactics, and tips for boosting accuracy and speed.

Online Safety Training Video Course

Meet the Handgun Safety Training requirements for many states with this easy-to-follow video and quiz. A certified firearms instructor will lead you through the basics of handgun ownership and safe handling while carrying concealed.

Shooting For Accuracy: Premium Marksmanship Training

Increase your shooting accuracy with expert training tips that you can put to use right away. A perfect guide for both new and experienced shooters, this resource demonstrates proper grip, firing stances, trigger squeeze instructions, and more to take your accuracy to the next level.

American Concealed Shot Training Correction Targets

Take your firing range practice to the next level with paper targets that diagnose common shooting mistakes and provide marksmanship tips to get your shots back on target. Available in packs of 3 on AmericanConcealed.com.

www.ingramcontent.com/pod-product-compliance
Lightning Source LLC
Chambersburg PA
CBHW050436010526
44118CB00013B/1552